low carb
super drinks

low carb
super drinks

michael van straten

MITCHELL BEAZLEY

Low Carb Super Drinks

by Michael van Straten

First published in Great Britain in 2005 by
Mitchell Beazley, an imprint of Octopus Publishing
Group Limited, 2–4 Heron Quays, London E14 4JP.

A CIP catalogue record for this book is available from the British Library.

ISBN: 1 84533 076 5

The author and publishers will be grateful for any information that will assist them in keeping
future editions up-to-date. Although all reasonable care has been taken in the preparation of this
book, neither the publishers, editors nor the author can accept any liability for any consequences
arising from the use thereof, or the information contained therein.

Commissioning Editors: Rebecca Spry/Vivien Antwi
Executive Art Editor: Yasia Williams
Design: Gaelle Lochner
Photographer: Peter Cassidy
Editor: Jamie Ambrose
Proof reader: Diona Gregory
Index: Sandra Shotter
Production: Seyhan Essen

Typeset in Myriad MM

Printed and bound by Toppan Printing Company in China

Contents

Introduction

This is a book of delicious and wonderfully health-giving drinks, every one of which is suitable to include in any family's daily diet. What makes these recipes unique is that they're all low in carbohydrates. If you're trying to lose weight or, more importantly, play an active role in the prevention of obesity in your children, these drinks will help. But this book isn't written just for would-be slimmers; all the recipes have either a valuable nutritional content or a specific therapeutic benefit – in many cases, both.

For those who need to shed some pounds, the formula for successful long-term weight control is to consume fewer calories, spend less time in front of the TV, computer or games console, and burn more calories through exercise. Extreme regimes, crash diets, and meal replacements never work as permanent solutions; they end up turning you into a yo-yo dieter, and every new scheme means you end up heavier than when you started because the way of life they require is unsustainable. The minute you quit, you put back all the pounds you lost – plus a few.

High-protein and very restricted carbohydrate diets were around long before Dr. Atkins. As a young practitioner in the Twiggy-inspired 1960s, and under considerable pressure from my female patients, I devised one of my own. Within months I abandoned it, as the side effects rapidly became apparent: ketosis (a disturbance of the body's chemistry), bad breath, and constipation; there was also the realization that my patients were consuming inordinately high amounts of health-damaging saturated fats, with all the attendant risks of high blood pressure, strokes, and heart disease. Today, scientific evidence has shown that this type of eating increases the rate of bone loss and the consequent likelihood of osteoporosis, and may also cause significant and irreversible kidney damage.

The drinks my wife and I have devised for this book are the ideal compromise. They provide a range of low-, very low-, and no-carbohydrate drinks to help control your total calorie consumption while still following a sensible, balanced weight-reduction regime. In these pages you'll find wonderful alternatives to commercial canned drinks, soda, squashes, smoothies, and cordials. Most take only minutes to prepare, and enable you and your family to avoid the eight teaspoons of sugar, enormous amounts of questionable artificial sweeteners, and all the chemical colourings, flavourings, preservatives, and thickeners that are widely used in the soft drink, commercial-smoothie, and milk-shake industries.

Homemade lemonades and cordials are perfect examples of how much better and healthier such drinks can be. You'll also find calcium- and protein-rich shakes and smoothies, herbal teas (which help everything from insomnia and sore throats to PMS, fluid retention, and arthritis), and drinks which are like soups in a cup: full of vitality, nutrients, healing enzymes, and infection-fighting immune-boosters. There are other benefits, thanks to the massive antioxidant content of some recipes. These high Oxygen Radical Absorbance Capacity (ORAC) ingredients are the most potent source of the natural elements that protect against heart disease, strokes, cancers, and ageing.

There's no doubt that there are both good and bad carbohydrates. The good ones are those you consume in a form that's as close as possible to the way Nature produced them: wholegrain cereals, naturally occurring fruit sugars, and soluble fibre from fruits and vegetables. Broadly speaking, carbs are divided into sugars and starches, but not all carbs are equal, as you'll soon discover if you start looking at food labels. "Sugars" may mean the natural fructose that occurs in fruits and some vegetables, or it could refer to commercially manufactured sucrose, dextrose, malto-dextrose, corn syrup, and many more.

All carbohydrates can be further classified according to their glycaemic index (GI): the measure of how quickly they're converted into sugars and trigger the body's release of insulin into the bloodstream. High-GI foods, such as glucose, white flour, and all refined carbohydrates, are rapidly turned to sugar and have an immediate impact on insulin levels. It's these high-GI items that increase the risk of obesity, insulin resistance, and Type-2 diabetes. Low-GI foods, like wholegrain cereals, vegetables, nuts, and seeds, are not only preferable but much healthier. For example, peanuts and peanut butter are an excellent aid to weight loss; like all low-GI foods, they produce slow, sustained energy release, so you don't feel hungry or get desperate sugar cravings soon after they're consumed. What's more, peanuts have been shown to reduce significantly the risk of developing Type-2 diabetes – as long as you eat them fresh, not salted or covered with chocolate.

Every recipe in this book has a low-carb star rating per portion/person: ***** for very low or no carbs; ** for low carbs; and * for moderately low carbs.**

Good health and enjoyment are here for you and your whole family. And of course, there's weight control, too, if you need it.

Brea

There's absolutely no arguing with the fact that breakfast is the most important meal of the day. Before eating it, you'll probably have spent longer without food than at any other time during a normal twenty-four hours, so your blood-sugar levels will be at their lowest ebb. This is where you refuel your body and energize it for the morning's work ahead. Most importantly, you're recharging your mental as well as physical resources. Getting it right now will make a huge difference to all areas of your performance,

kfast

Drinks

whether it's studying, accounting, bricklaying, gardening, or coping with one of the most complex tasks of all: running a house and family. All the drinks in this section provide a bonus of super-nutrients and protective phytochemicals. Add complex carbohydrates such as wholemeal bread or a good breakfast cereal, and you have the ideal breakfast. Slow-release energy in the morning, with a modest amount of protein, is all the body requires for optimum function until lunchtime.

C U Soon

Since it is also cleansing, cooling, and mildly diuretic, lettuce makes this low-carb juice an ideal tonic for the digestive system, eyes, and skin.

Serves 1–2

3 unpeeled carrots;
unless organic, remove top
and bottom
1 small bunch of chives
1 small bunch of coriander
1 (smallish) cos lettuce

1 Wash all the ingredients well and put them through a juicer, reserving a few of the chives.
2 Mix the juice well.
3 Snip the reserved chives with scissors and scatter on top of the juice to serve.

vital statistics and low carb low-down

The calorie-conscious know that lettuce is ninety-five per cent water and has hardly any **calories**, yet its nutritional value is enough to surprise anyone. Nearly **starch-free** and with just a little **natural sugar** from the carrots, this moderately **low-carb** drink is super-rich in **vitamin A** and **carotenoids** and a rich source of **potassium** and **folic acid**. It also contains useful amounts of **vitamin C, B** vitamins, **iron**, and **iodine**. The **antiseptic** and **antifungal** sulphur compounds in the chives, the **diuretic** and **calming** oils in lettuce, and the unique **digestion-promoting** constituents of coriander make it a highly potent **cleansing** mixture.

Get Up and Go

low carb rating:

Here is a start-the-day juice with a vengeance. Make sure you choose the ripest-possible tomatoes, as that's when they're at their most nutritious. Most people don't realize that tomatoes are a member of the *Solanaceae* family, which includes potatoes, peppers, and aubergines: they're all relatives of the nightshades. For this reason, this juice is not ideal for anyone with rheumatoid arthritis, though it's not a problem if you have osteoarthritis. To make it, stir the kelp powder (you can find it in most good health-food shops) into the juice just before drinking.

Serves 1–2

4 medium tomatoes
30g or 1oz fresh root ginger
2 celery sticks, with leaves
1 small sweet potato, unpeeled
2 tsp kelp powder

1 Wash the first four ingredients and put them through a juicer.
2 Mix the juice well.
3 Stir in the kelp powder.

vital statistics and low carb low-down

Although they're starchy, sweet potatoes are nutritionally **valuable**. This drink is super-rich in **vitamin C**, betacarotene, **lycopene**, and **iodine**, and also contain **potassium** and folic acid. As well as all the **protective** benefits of the **carotenoids** and vitamin C, this juice also contains some **coumarin** compounds from the celery, which pep up the entire circulatory system, boost the **protective** function of white cells, and **lower blood pressure.** The kelp powder is rich in **iodine**, which stimulates the thyroid and gets your body working in **overdrive**. Just what you need at the start of the day!

Wake Up Tommy

low carb rating:

When you've been laid low by a cold or flu, you're recovering from illness or an operation, or you're just ground down by an extended period of work or stress, this is the drink you need. Packed with vitality, energy, and valuable nutrients, you'll find this tomato-based, almost soup-like beverage an instant shot in the arm. Easily digested and with a savoury tang to please even the most jaded of palates, it will soon be on your list of favourite breakfast drinks.

Serves 4
300ml or 10½fl oz vegetable stock (see recipe for Veggie Mug on page 97 or make it with a low-salt commercial stock cube)
200ml or 7fl oz milk
1 x 400g or 14oz can tinned crushed tomatoes
1 large onion, peeled and finely grated
20g or ¾ oz sago

1 Put all the ingredients into a large pot or saucepan.
2 Simmer for one hour.
3 Strain and serve in mugs.

vital statistics and low carb low-down

Tomatoes are the richest of all sources of the nutrient lycopene. This member of the carotenoid family is one of the most protective of all the phytochemicals and will quickly boost your lowered vitality. Sago, made from the starchy pith of the sago palm tree, is a quickly digested energy source, providing very small amounts of complex carbohydrates. Minerals from the vegetable stock, and calcium and B vitamins from the milk, add to the energy-boosting value.

Eye Opener

low carb rating:

In these days of computers, VDUs, and TV, it has never been more important to protect the eyes. The most common cause of poor sight and blindness in elderly people is age-related macular degeneration, or AMD. The latest evidence shows that this disease tends to coincide with a low intake of specific carotenoids. People who consistently eat foods containing these protective substances are at much lower risk of getting AMD.

Serves 2

4 unpeeled carrots; unless organic, remove top and bottom

1 bunch of watercress

2 kale leaves

1 handful of spinach leaves

1 small handful of parsley, with stems

1 Wash all the ingredients and put them through a juicer.
2 Stir well before serving.

vital statistics and low carb low-down

The perfect breakfast if you're off to the office, college or school to spend a day in front of a computer screen. This **low-carb** drink is **super-rich** in **vitamin A**, betacarotene, and other essential **carotenoids**. Contains vitamins C and E, **folic acid**, and **iron**. The old wives' tale that carrots help you see in the dark is true. **Betacarotene** is essential for proper **night vision**, and other carotenoids, such as **lutein** and **xeaxanthine** in spinach and kale, also protect against age-related macular degeneration. This is a juice to drink regularly for long-term **eye health** and **protection**.

Carrot and Coriander Blitz

low carb rating:

★ ☆

The winning partnership of carrots with coriander makes a wonderfully hearty and healthy soup, but it also makes a great breakfast drink. Here's a quick way to get all the benefits of this often taken-for-granted vegetable and the fabulously peppery taste of fresh coriander, which is available year-round in most supermarkets these days. This drink takes just minutes to make, and it's full of fibre, vitamins, and minerals. As well as being filling (but without loads of calories), it give your blood a boost, too.

Serves 2

500ml or 18fl oz carrot juice. It's FAR cheaper to make your own juice from this readily available and great-value vegetable, but a good commercial brand will work just as well

1 tsp ground coriander

2 handfuls of fresh coriander

1 Put the carrot juice into a saucepan.
2 Add the ground coriander.
3 Wash the fresh coriander, tear roughly, and add to the pan.
4 Heat through, then simmer for five minutes, stirring gently.
5 Remove the coriander leaves with a slotted spoon before serving.

vital statistics and low carb low-down

There's very little starch in carrots, but there are some **natural** sugars. Using carrot juice removes some of the starch, resulting in this **health-giving low-carb** drink. It's better to used "old" rather than "new" carrots here as they have a much higher content of **circulation-boosting** betacarotene. As the carrots mature and their colour deepens, so the levels of this nutrient rise. Both coriander seeds and leaves help boost the circulation, thanks to their **linalool**, **alpha-pinene**, and **coriandrol** content. Do be careful with the seeds, however – especially if you're getting them from your own plants. When unripe, they both taste and smell horrible. After you've gathered them, store them in an airtight jar for at least a month before using.

Peach of a Drink

low carb rating:

This yoghurt smoothie is deliciously nutritious. It's rich in youth-preserving antioxidants. It also serves to boost your immune system, and as a bonus, the hormone-like substances in soya yoghurt will help even out the ups and downs of hormones. Even if you're not that keen on soya products, you could add much more of the yoghurt to this drink, as the flavour will be disguised by the fruits.

Serves 1–2
4 ready-to-eat dried apricots
1 large, ripe peach
2 large oranges
30ml or 1fl oz soya yoghurt

1 Soak the apricots (even if they're "ready to eat") for thirty minutes in just enough freshly boiled water to cover them.
2 Wash and halve the peach, remove the stone, and put the flesh into a blender.
3 Squeeze the juice from the oranges and add to the peach flesh.
4 Drain the apricots, add to the blender, and whizz until smooth.
5 Add the yoghurt and whizz again briefly.

vital statistics and low carb low-down

With virtually **no starch** and a very **low glycemic index**, this is an ideal breakfast drink for carb watchers. Dried apricots are an exceptional source of **betacarotene**, some of which the body uses as a natural **protective** antioxidant and some of which is converted into **vitamin A**. They are extremely rich in **fibre**, too, and an excellent source of **iron**. The peach also contributes betacarotene, while the oranges supply twice the daily requirement of **vitamin C**. Isoflavones (hormone-like substances) are found in all soya products and are **helpful** for PMS, hot flushes during the menopause, and for **protection** against osteoporosis.

Apple Power

A zappy cleanser to start your day, Apple Power is ideal for stimulating the digestive system and replacing lost minerals following physical activity – on or off the sports field. Take this on an empty stomach and don't eat or drink anything else for half an hour to let its natural fruit sugars do their work.

Serves 1–2

2 large Granny Smith apples, unpeeled, uncored, and quartered

1 peeled lime (or unpeeled key lime)

6 sorrel leaves

1 sprig of mint, with stems

1 handful of parsley, with stems

1 Wash all the ingredients and put them through a juicer.
2 Mix well before serving.

vital statistics and low carb low-down

Here's a very **low-carb** start to your day, but it's not enough on its own for breakfast: you'll need a protein dish like a poached egg or a piece of cheese with rye bread or rice crackers to complete your meal. Nevertheless, this drink is **super-rich in vitamins A, C, E, B$_6$,** and **folic acid**, rich in **magnesium** and **potassium**, and contains some calcium and **iron**. Soluble fibre in apples and **natural oils** in mint have a wonderful effect on the entire digestive system, as they are **soothing** and cause a gentle laxative effect. Sorrel has been used by Native Americans for centuries as an **anti-cancer** herb; the lime's natural pigment, known as **limonene**, protects against cancer, too. Try this one for some real health power in a glass.

Tangy Bananas

Don't knock it until you've tried it. This may sound like a crazy hybrid somewhere between a Virgin Bloody Mary and a banana split, but this unlikely mixture tastes extraordinarily good. Many people find the idea of warm tomato juice very strange, but no-one raises an eyebrow at the thought of hot tomato soup. If you feel in need of a fillip at the beginning of the day and you like the ingredients separately, surprise yourself with this drink.

Serves 2
2 small bananas, peeled
500ml or 18fl oz tomato juice
2 shakes of Worcestershire sauce

1 In a small blender, purée the bananas with a little of the tomato juice until very smooth.
2 Put the rest of the juice in a saucepan.
3 Add the banana pulp and warm gently, stirring continuously.
4 Pour into mugs.
5 Serve with the shakes of Worcestershire sauce on top.

vital statistics and low carb low-down

The health benefits of bananas far outweigh their **modest carbohydrate** content. This is instant **pick-up power** by the mugful. Whether it's chronic fatigue, hormonal ups and downs, too many late nights, or overdoing things at work, bananas contain the **B vitamins**, **potassium**, **fibre**, and easily released **energy** that you need. Add the lycopene for super **protection** from the tomatoes and the **stimulating**, spicy zing from Worcestershire sauce and you're ready to face the day.

Jungle Smoothie

low carb rating:

Make this a family favourite for breakfast and you'll send them all off to school, college, or work with a shot in the arm for their natural resistance. This is really valuable during the autumn and winter months, when we are all exposed to other people's flu- and cold-causing organisms. It makes a great sustaining smoothie for when it's going to be a long time before the next meal, and a perfect pre-exercise recipe when you can't eat a meal but need some extra energy and stamina.

Serves 2
1 large mango
2 bananas
400ml or 14fl oz plain live yoghurt

1 Peel, stone, and cube the mango.
2 Peel and slice the bananas.
3 Put all the ingredients into a blender and whizz until smooth.

vital statistics and low carb low-down
With its very **low glycemic index rating** and only a small amount of starch from the bananas, this is a **resistance-building** start to the day. It's rich in **betacarotene**, flavonoids, potassium, **antioxidants**, and **vitamin C** from the mango; plenty of **potassium**, fast- and slow-release **energy**, and **vitamin B$_6$** from the bananas, and more resistance-building bacteria from the yoghurt. Peeling the mango is well worth the effort.

Morning Power Pack

low carb rating:

This juice may not win friends and influence people, and it is not for the faint-hearted, but Morning Power Pack represents the ultimate in veggie power. It is a juice which exploits the pick of the protective vegetables with the kick of garlic, mooli, and jalapeño. An all-year-round immune booster with massive built-in protection, it tastes seriously better than it sounds – but make sure you drink it with the one you love.

Serves 1–2

1 garlic clove, peeled

2 unpeeled carrots; unless organic, remove top and bottom

1 medium tomato

1 sweet potato, scrubbed, unpeeled and cut into sticks

1 jalapeño pepper, deseeded

1 stick celery, with leaves

3 inches mooli (white radish)

1   Wash all the ingredients and put them through a juicer.
2   Mix well before serving.

vital statistics and low carb low-down

This amazing all-round health package is well worth the few carbohydrates from the carrots and sweet potato. It's **super-rich** in **vitamins A, C,** and **E,** carotenoids, and **potassium** and rich in **vitamin B$_6$,** folic acid, **magnesium,** iron, and other **B vitamins.** This is breakfast in a glass, but it's not just the conventional nutrients that make it so valuable. The enormous **protective benefits** of garlic can help prevent heart, **circulation,** chest, and other bacteria and fungi infections. Ginger also protects the **heart** and, together with the jalapeño pepper, the **joints,** too. Mooli, the white radish, is one of the great **liver** protectors.

Spicy Spinach

low carb rating:

The common expression "to ginger you up" isn't just a coincidence, because ginger has been used as a physical and circulatory stimulant since the ancient Chinese physicians were practising 5,000 years ago. Teamed here with the legendary power-pack of spinach, this is another soup-like drink that is sure to give you a breakfast-time boost.

Serves 2
905g or 2lb baby spinach leaves
1 tsp ground ginger
 plus 2 small pinches , for decoration
200g or 7oz low-fat fromage frais
300ml or 10½fl oz skimmed milk

1 Wash the spinach and put in a saucepan with only the water that is clinging to it.
2 Stir in the ginger.
3 Put over a low heat until the spinach is wilted.
4 Tip into a blender, add the fromage frais, and whizz until smooth.
5 Put back into the pan, add the skimmed milk, and heat through.
6 Serve with the extra ginger sprinkled on top.

vital statistics and low carb low-down

Almost **starch-free**, this is a delicious **low-carb** start to the day. Essential oils in ginger dilate the tiny blood vessels, **warming** the skin and speeding up the **circulation**. The huge quantities of **carotenoids** in spinach are a gift to all the body's **protective** mechanisms, and the large quantities of **calcium** in this drink are not only bone-protective, but also help improve the passage of **nerve impulses**, control blood pressure, and maintain effective **heart function**.

Prune Relish

low carb rating:

☆ ☆

You can enjoy the complex flavours of this recipe as a thickish juice or as a really thick smoothie, depending on your taste. But however you like it, the prunes, apples, and grapes will greatly enhance your body's restorative powers. Adding the cheese makes it quite substantial and a valuable source of body-building nutrients for anyone under the weather.

Serves 1–2
10 pitted, ready-to-eat prunes
1 large dessert apple
255g or 9oz white seedless grapes
115ml or 4fl oz mascarpone cheese
still mineral water

1 Put the prunes into a bowl, just cover with freshly boiled water, and leave to soak for thirty minutes.
2 Meanwhile, wash the apple and grapes. Core and quarter the apple and put it through a juicer with the grapes, saving a few grapes for decoration.
3 Put the juice into a blender.
4 Drain the prunes and add them to the juice.
5 Whizz until smooth.
6 Add the mascarpone and whizz again.
7 If the mixture seems too thick for your taste, add mineral water until you get the required consistency.
8 Serve with the grapes floating on top.

vital statistics and low carb low-down

Even though it tastes sweet, the starch content is extremely low and the **energy** content high. What more do you need for breakfast? The prunes alone in this recipe provide huge amounts of **protective antioxidants** – in fact, enough to see you right through the day. The natural sugars from the grapes and the **cholesterol-lowering** pectins in the apple juice just add to the **beneficial** nutritional properties that you'll get in every glass. Include the **calcium**, **zinc**, and **protein** from the mascarpone, and you've got a drink fit for a king.

Fruity Wake-Up Call

low carb rating:

When peeling the grapefruit and oranges to make this fruit-packed juice, be sure to leave plenty of the white pith still attached to the flesh, as this is where this tonic's bioflavonoids are found. If you're lucky enough to find very thin-skinned lemons, there's no need to peel them at all – though it's best to taste a little of the peel first, as it can sometimes be very bitter.

Serves 2

1 unwaxed lemon, with peel if thin-skinned

2 oranges, peeled and pith removed

2 grapefruit*, peeled and pith removed

*If taking prescribed medicines, consult your doctor before drinking large amounts of grapefruit juice.

1   Put all the ingredients through a juicer*.
2   Mix well before serving.

*If you don't have a large electric juicer, juice the fruit with a hand-held device. You'll lose some of the nutrients, but Fruity Wake-Up Call will still taste delicious.

vital statistics and low carb low-down

This **moderately low-carb** drink is **super-rich** in **vitamin C** and **potassium** and also contains useful amounts of **calcium**. It's not just the vitamin C content that is so important in this recipe, it's the wide range of protective **flavonoids** which helps **increase natural immunity** against both bacteria and viruses and plays a major part in **protecting** the body against cancer. As a bonus, you'll also get a substantial shot of **folic acid** and some useful **vitamin A**.

Quince Tea

low carb rating:

☆ ☆ ☆

You may have to hunt around a bit to find quince jelly, but there are specialist manufacturers who supply the very best food shops and delicatessens with this wonderful, clean-tasting preserve that was such a favourite in medieval and Victorian England. You'll also find nasturtium flowers offered as food in certain supermarkets – and in any garden centre you care to mention. And, of course, you could just grow your own.

Serves 2
2 Earl Grey tea bags
2 heaped tsp quince jelly
2 nasturtium flowers

1 Make the tea in individual mugs.
2 While the tea is still piping hot, cut the quince jelly into small pieces and stir vigorously into the tea.
3 Serve with the washed nasturtium flowers floating on top.

vital statistics and low carb low-down

The small amount of sugar in a teaspoon of quince jelly is insignificant in this otherwise **carb-free drink**. Bergamot gives the unmistakable flavour to Earl Grey tea, and its **heady** aroma instantly adds a touch of **romance**. When accompanied by the sharp, **peppery** flavour of the nasturtium flowers and the **sensual** taste of the quince, this drink is ideal for a lazy Sunday brunch.

Refr

As soon as the sun shines, the epidemic starts. Wherever you look, there's a rash spreading across the country of people swigging fizzy drinks from cans. I can't imagine anything less refreshing than swallowing mouthfuls of cloyingly sweet, coloured water filled with sugar, sweeteners, flavourings, and destructive chemicals. The average can of cola drink contains around ten teaspoons of sugar – and if you think you're better off with sugar-free, diet or "lite" versions, think again. Most six-year-olds are consuming more artificial sweeteners each day than the recommended safe intake for an adult, and there are experts who question the long-term safety of some of these chemicals. Behavioural problems, rotten teeth, obesity, and diabetes are serious enough consequences of high sugar consumption, but many of these drinks also cause loss of calcium from bones and are a major factor in the development of osteoporosis in later life. What makes these particular health problems even more appalling is the fact that they're preventable.

shing

Drinks

If you want a drink that's healthy and refreshing for you or your children, don't turn to the cans and bottles on supermarket shelves: just turn the pages of this chapter. Here you'll find super low-carb drinks which are far more refreshing – and every single one simply oozes with nutrients and positive health benefits. Yes, they take a little time and trouble to make, but they're infinitely superior; they can also save you lots of money as they're far less expensive than buying ready-made commercial products. With these recipes, you can make simple teas, your own scented lemonade drinks, fabulous fresh juices, and wonderful, healthy things for the youngsters such as a blueberry and raspberry crush or a melon and strawberry drink. You can also indulge in the exotic pleasures of tropical fruits such as mangoes and pineapples or even the slightly bizarre-sounding mixture of carrots, apples, radishes, lemon, beetroot, and sauerkraut – yes, you really *can* get delicious juice from pickled cabbage.

Scented Lemonade

low carb rating:

In England, lemonade has traditionally been a drink for children or invalids. This version owes more to the American Deep South, where it was served to those wonderful Southern belles on the verandah in the cooling breeze of a stifling afternoon. An invitation to share a jug of this seemingly innocent brew often meant much more to those who could read between the lines of impeccable Southern manners. Quite frankly, you *will* give a damn once you've tasted this!

Serves 2
2 tsp golden caster sugar
2 cloves
¼ tsp ground cinnamon
1 unwaxed lemon
6 scented geranium leaves

1. Put the sugar, cloves, and cinnamon into a saucepan along with 500ml or 18fl oz water.
2. Bring slowly to a boil.
3. Juice the lemon and reserve two thin twists of peel.
4. Add the juice to the pan and bring it back to a boil.
5. Take the geranium leaves off their stalks, wash and add to the pan, cover, and leave for five minutes off the heat.
6. Strain.
7. Serve warm or cold with the lemon twists on top.

vital statistics and low carb low-down

The Spice Island flavours of cloves and cinnamon are really outclassed by their **aromatic oils**. The **mild** and **relaxing** benefits of cinnamon combine with the **sensually stimulating** eugenol of cloves, and the final touch is the delicate **aphrodisiac** effect of scented geranium.

Colour Me Cool

low carb rating:

This mixture of orange, pink, green, and yellow citrus fruits is both a liver and intestinal cleanser. Its clean, tangy, wide-awake taste also makes it a favourite anytime refreshing drink. Use this juice as an excellent start to a detox cleansing day. And if you're unfortunate enough to wake up with a hangover, this cocktail works better than the hair of any dog.

Serves 3–4
2 oranges, peeled but with pith
1 unwaxed lemon, with peel if thin-
   skinned
1 lime, peeled
1 pink grapefruit*, peeled, leaving
   pith behind

*If taking prescribed medicines, consult
your doctor before drinking large
amounts of grapefruit juice.

1   Put all the fruit through a juicer*.
2   Mix thoroughly together to serve.`

*If you don't have a large electric juicer, juice the fruits with a hand-held device.

vital statistics and low carb low-down

Super-rich in **vitamin C**. Rich in **vitamin A**. Contains a useful amount of **potassium** and **calcium**. The acidity of all these citric juices helps remove some of the unwanted bacteria from the digestive tract and **encourages** the growth of **beneficial** probiotic bacteria. Besides tasting terrific, this refreshing drink is also a good **aid** to **digestion**. Drink it for two or three days after a course of antibiotics to get your system back in good running order.

Rosemaryade

Lemons are one of the traditional ingredients of fasting and detoxing regimes. Their juice is cleansing and mildly diuretic, and this unusual recipe for lemonade produces four large glasses of deliciously cleansing juice. The rosemary helps boost your mood and improves the memory. If you haven't got a rosemary bush in your garden, now's the time to get one, even if it is just in a pot on your doorstep, where it will grow very happily all year round. A brilliantly refreshing drink – and slimming, too. What more could you ask for in a low-carb life?

Serves 4

3 lemons

2 tsp brown sugar

3 sprigs of rosemary, washed

400ml or 14fl oz ordinary tap water

850ml or 30fl oz sparkling mineral water

1 Wash the lemons. Grate off the rind and put it into a saucepan with the sugar, rosemary, and tap water.
2 Bring slowly to the boil, simmer for ten minutes, and cool slightly.
3 Add the juice of the lemons.
4 Leave until cold.
5 Strain and add mineral water before serving.

vital statistics and low carb low-down

This drink is infinitely healthier than any slimming drink you could buy. Most of the **vitamin C** from the lemons is preserved in this drink, as the juice is added after boiling. It also supplies **bioflavonoids** from the peel as well as the intriguing flavour of rosemary mingled with the tangy taste of the lemons. Rosemary contains **volatile oils** and flavonoids that have a direct and **beneficial effect** on the **brain**.

Parsley and Lemon Tea

low carb rating:

At first glance, this refreshing concoction may seem an unlikely combination, but parsley tea with lemon isn't really any different from Indian tea with lemon. Parsley is a great favourite with traditional herbalists, although it is much ignored by the general public. Yet it's so much more than just a mild flavouring or an attractive garnish. I fear that far more parsley goes back to the kitchens than ever gets eaten. It has wonderful protective properties – as do the lemons in this recipe, which are a rich source of immune-boosting vitamin C and bioflavonoids.

Serves 2
3 unwaxed lemons
1 large bunch of parsley
2 tsp golden caster sugar

1 Peel the rind, but not the pith, off the lemons.
2 Wash and roughly tear the parsley.
3 Put the lemon rind and parsley into a saucepan with the sugar and 340ml or 12fl oz water.
4 Bring slowly to the boil, stirring to ensure the sugar is dissolved.
5 Simmer for five minutes and strain.
6 Juice the lemons and stir in the juice to serve.

vital statistics and low carb low-down

Parsley is rich in the **protective vitamins A** and **C** and also contains **blood-building iron**, bone-strengthening **calcium**, and **heart-protective** potassium. Additionally, this favourite herb of the ancient Greeks and Romans is also a **mild diuretic**, helping to **protect** the kidneys and prevent high blood pressure. Because it **improves** the way in which the body eliminates uric acid, parsley also protects against arthritis, rheumatism, and gout.

Hot Citrus Ginger

low carb rating:

Whether you choose to enjoy this hot or cold, it's equally refreshing. The sweetness of the grapes and oranges, the tartness of the lemon and lime, and the hint of fiery ginger all combine to produce an intriguing flavour that instantly cleanses and refreshes the palate and alerts the mind. Summer or winter, you'll be refreshed and healthier after a glass of this super low-carb drink.

Serves 2

1 lemon
1 lime
2 oranges
15g or ½ oz fresh root ginger
170g or 6oz white grapes

1 Peel the lemon and lime, removing the pith.
2 Peel the oranges, leaving the pith.
3 Grate the ginger.
4 Wash the grapes.
5 Put all the ingredients through a juicer.
6 Mix well before serving.

vital statistics and low carb low-down

Super-rich in **vitamin C** and **bioflavonoids**. Contains **carotenoids** and **calcium**. As well as the **immune-boosting**, **defensive** properties of the very high vitamin C content, this delicious juice also contains **gingerols** from the ginger, which **stimulate** the **circulation** and produce a strong expectorant effect that helps if you've got a cough.

Strawbs With a Twist

low carb rating:

The first time I saw my wife grind black pepper over her strawberries I thought she'd finally flipped. But once I tasted this traditional Mediterranean culinary trick, I realized why people did it. The pepper somehow magnifies the flavour of strawberries and makes them even more delicious. Combining that taste with luscious, ripe melon makes this a memorable drink. Because you're using the whole fruit, it's filling and substantial: a perfect mid-morning or mid-afternoon sustaining and refreshing snack.

Serves 1–2
1 cantaloup melon
225g or 8oz strawberries
still mineral water
freshly ground black pepper

1 Peel and deseed the melon.
2 Wash and hull the strawberries.
3 Put them both into a blender and whizz until smooth.
4 Thin to the desired consistency with mineral water.
5 Serve with a few twists of pepper in each glass.

vital statistics and low carb low-down

Melon is a good source of **folic acid**, **potassium**, and **vitamins**. The strawberries not only provide generous quantities of **betacarotene**, they're also valuable in the **relief** of **arthritic pain**. Contrary to popular myth which says they're acidic and bad for people with joint problems, they are really **beneficial**. This drink is a good source of **fibre** and **quick-release energy**, thanks to the natural fruit sugars that are abundant in these two fruits.

Smoothie Operator

low carb rating:

Just the aroma of mango, pineapple, lime, and ginger is a transport to paradise. Drinking these juices is a passport to long-term good health and vitality. Whipped into a cooling, frothy shake with live yoghurt, this combination is invigorating, refreshing, and protective. It's wonderful for children (though they may prefer it without the ginger) and perfect in the early stages of pregnancy, as ginger helps prevent and relieve morning sickness.

Serves 3–4
1 mango
1 pineapple
1 lime
30g or 1oz fresh root ginger
140ml or 5fl oz live low-fat yoghurt
a handful of ice cubes

1 Peel and stone the mango.
2 Cut the top off the pineapple to peel it.
3 Peel the lime.
4 Juice all three fruits, plus the ginger, and put into a blender.
5 Add the yoghurt and ice cubes and blitz until you have a crush.

vital statistics and low carb low-down

Super-rich in **vitamins A, C,** and **bioflavonoids**. Rich in **calcium**. Contains some **B vitamins, phosphorus, copper, iron,** and **magnesium**. The **healing** enzyme **bromelain** in the pineapple, the **vitamin A** in the mango, and vitamin C with bioflavonoids in the lime make this one of the most comprehensive **protectors** around. Add the **beneficial bacteria** in yoghurt, and you'll see why Smoothie Operator is one of the **healthiest low-carb drinks**.

Stone Me!

low carb rating:

Instant sunshine, instant energy, instant pleasure, and instantly refreshing, this low-carb drink is also instantly protective. It's good for your digestion, great for the skin, and will also give your immune system a shot in the arm. The orange flesh of apricots and peaches is a rich source of betacarotene, and the mango provides even more of this vital nutrient. And everyone knows about the vitamin C in oranges.

Serves 4
6 apricots
6 peaches
1 mango
2 oranges

1 Wash and stone the apricots and peaches.
2 Peel and stone the mango.
3 Peel the oranges, keeping the pith.
4 Put all the fruit through a juicer.
5 Mix well and chill to serve.

vital statistics and low carb low-down
Super-rich in **vitamins A** and **C**. Contains **potassium**, **calcium**, and **magnesium**. Although this juice has **valuable** vitamins, it's really the **enzymes** and **protective chemicals** that make it such **good health** news. Besides its other benefits, it is helpful in **fighting** chest **infections** and is also **good** for anyone with high **blood pressure**.

Lemon and Ginger Cup

low carb rating:

My mother always used to say that there's nothing more refreshing on a summer's day than a nice cup of tea. As a child, I found this very hard to understand. Now I know better – this perfect combination of ginger and lemon makes one of the most refreshing hot drinks you'll ever taste. Of course, it's equally comforting and warming on the coldest winter's day.

Serves 1
2.5cm or 1 inch fresh root ginger
half an unwaxed lemon

1 Peel and grate the ginger.
2 Put into an infuser or mug.
3 Add 200ml or 7fl oz of boiling water.
4 Cover and leave for ten minutes.
5 Juice the lemon, reserving two slices.
6 Strain the ginger tea into a mug and add the lemon juice.
7 Serve with the lemon slices on top.

vital statistics and low carb low-down

While we in the West consider ginger to be a warming, tangy spice that adds its wonderful flavour to both sweet and savoury dishes, Chinese herbalists have very different ideas. For 7,000 years, they've used it as an important medicine as well as a flavouring. The pungent **shogaols** and the **stimulating gingerols** and **zingiberene** have a dramatic effect on blood circulation, making this root a great **remedy** for poor **circulation**, chilblains, and Raynaud's disease. The **bioflavonoids** in lemon help by **strengthening** the **blood vessel** walls. And as a bonus, it contains **zero carbs**.

Fresh Tomato Juice

low carb rating:

Once you've tasted this refreshing drink, it's unlikely you'll ever enjoy the commercial varieties again. Whether in cans or cartons, these nearly always have added salt and lack the sweet and sour flavour of the freshly juiced fruits. The acidity of tomatoes is cleansing – even more so when combined with the diuretic properties of celery and the overall detoxing power of garlic. The Worcestershire sauce adds the bite, and if you really want the sting in the tail, why not pour in a measure of vodka?

Serves 2

10 ripe tomatoes
4 celery stalks, with leaves
1 small garlic clove
2 dashes Worcestershire sauce

1. Put the tomatoes into a large bowl.
2. Cover with boiling water and leave until cool enough to handle.
3. Slip off the skins.
4. Wash the celery and chop roughly, reserving two sprigs of leaves.
5. Peel the garlic clove.
6. Put all the ingredients through a juicer.
7. Add the Worcestershire sauce and stir.
8. Chill in the refrigerator.
9. Serve with the reserved celery leaves on top.

vital statistics and low carb low-down

Ripe tomatoes are the **richest** source of the carotenoid **lycopene**, which is highly **protective** against heart disease and prostate cancer. This drink also supplies **betacarotene**, lots of **potassium**, and **vitamins C** and **E**. You'll get more potassium and some vitamin C from the celery as well as the **natural diuretics** which this vegetable contains.

Laid-Back Spice

This ultra-refreshing drink contains coriander, one of the most ancient culinary and medicinal plants. Over the past 3,500 years, its use has spread from ancient Egypt and China, through Asia, North Africa, and into Europe, where it has long had a reputation as an aphrodisiac. Make sure you choose a ripe pineapple: it will feel heavy for its size if it's in perfect condition. Pulling the spiky leaves out of the top is no indication of its ripeness – that's just another old wives' tale.

Serves 1–2
half a peeled and washed pineapple
15g or ¹⁄₂ oz fresh root ginger
1 small bunch of coriander, washed

1 Cut the leaves off the pineapple.
2 Put through a juicer with the ginger and coriander.
3 Stir well to serve.

vital statistics and low carb low-down
Super-rich in **vitamin C**. Rich in potassium. Full of **healing** and **stimulating** enzymes, this spicy drink gets its punch from the **volatile oils** of ginger and the **flavonoids**, **coumarins**, and other plant chemicals found in coriander. The contrasting flavours of pineapple and ginger, together with the powerful **phytochemicals** present in coriander, give this juice a surprising but nonetheless delicious flavour.

Raspberry and Blueberry Slush

low carb rating:

One serving will give you more protection from the ravages of free radicals than most people get in three days from the average American, Northern European or UK diet. It's the free radicals that attack the body's individual cells, and it's this dangerous chemical activity that's frequently the trigger for heart disease, joint problems, diminishing eyesight, and cancer. Although you will certainly lose some of the vitamin C content from both fruits if they're frozen, the protective antioxidants aren't damaged, so you can enjoy this drink all year round.

Serves 1–2
200g or 7oz blueberries
200g or 7oz raspberries
crushed ice

1 Wash and hull the fruit.
2 Put it all into a blender and whizz until smooth.
3 Serve in long glasses over the crushed ice.

vital statistics and low carb low-down

Although there's virtually no starch in this wonderfully refreshing drink, it does contain natural fruit sugar, giving it its two-star low-carb rating. This is a **vitamin C**-rich recipe, but much more important for its exceptionally high **ORAC** score. ORAC stands for oxygen radical absorption capacity, a measure of food's ability to **neutralize** free radicals and **protect** the body from **ageing**, heart disease, **cancer**, and other degenerative conditions. The optimum ORAC score for a day is 5,000, but the average in the UK is barely 1,500. A large glass of this provides almost 6,000 ORACs.

Veggie Lemon Surprise

low carb rating:

Sauerkraut might sound like a strange thing to juice, but this pickled cabbage is used as a traditional East European protective medicine against stomach ulcers and cancer. Combining it with the cancer-fighting properties of beetroot and carrots, as well as the apple's natural pectin fibre (which protects the heart and circulation), makes this refreshing juice very special. It tastes much better than it sounds, too, since the sauerkraut's slightly acidic flavour is offset by the sweetness of the other ingredients.

Serves 4

3 unpeeled carrots, remove top and bottom unless organic

2 apples, quartered

1 unwaxed lemon, with peel if thin-skinned

1 medium beetroot, with leaves if possible

3 medium radishes, with leaves if possible

2 tbsp sauerkraut

1 Wash all the ingredients except the sauerkraut.
2 Put all the ingredients through a juicer.
3 Mix well before serving.

vital statistics and low carb low-down

Super-rich in **betacarotene**, **vitamin C**, **potassium**, and **folic acid**. Contains **calcium** and **iron**. The massive **potassium** content of beetroot with its leaves helps keep blood pressure low – vital for a long and active life. The radishes are specifically **healing** to the mucous membranes of the nose, **sinuses**, and **throat** and also **protect** against **chest infections**.

Gingered Up

low carb rating:

Ginger is a vital ingredient in ancient Chinese medicine and the traditional Ayurvedic healing of India. As well as its powerful medicinal actions, ginger is immensely stimulating. When we use the expression "to ginger someone up", we're invoking the genuine properties of this wonderful root.

Serves 1
1cm or ½ inch fresh ginger root
¼ large watermelon, with seeds and skin

1. Wash the watermelon.
2. Put both ingredients through a juicer.
3. Sieve if necessary to remove the watermelon seeds.
4. Mix well to serve.

vital statistics and low carb low-down

Combined with the refreshing, **energizing** properties of watermelon, this is one of the simplest yet healthiest **low-carb** juices. It contains small amounts of **vitamins A, C**, and **E**, but this juice isn't included in this book purely for its nutritional value. It does contain traces of vitamins, but these are not significant; its **enzymes** and gentle **diuretic** substances are its true assets. Ginger contains substances called **gingerol** and **zingiberene**, which dilate the blood vessels and **improve circulation**.

High-

In this twenty-first century, twenty-four/seven world, chronic fatigue, lethargy, and exhaustion are among the most common reasons for seeing your doctor. A life of never-ending hustle, bustle, and rush takes its toll and is also a prime reason for poor nutrition. Despite twenty-four-hour supermarkets and Sunday shopping, many people just don't find time to plan their eating and shop for the necessary ingredients. The result: take-aways, ready meals, convenience foods, instant soups, pot noodles, and a burger-bar attitude to food. This inevitably leads to overeating and undernourishment. Nutritional deficiencies are widespread, and even in affluent households, men, women, and children are more likely than not to be short of iron, zinc, calcium, selenium, vitamins A, D, E, folic acid, and –

nergy

Drinks

incredible though it may sound – even vitamin C. Apart from the disastrous effect that missing these nutrients has on immunity, anaemia, bone health, and heart and circulatory disease, some of them play vital roles in the conversion, storage, and availability of energy. All the drinks in this chapter are included because they either provide energy in its healthiest form or they enable the conversion of food into energy through the body's natural chemical processes. Use these delicious and sometimes unusual recipes to boost your nutrient levels, restore your vitality, and provide that extra energy boost when you need it. Taken regularly, they'll help you banish forever the spectre of tired-all-the-time syndrome.

Kiwi and Banana Smoothie

low carb rating:

Weight for weight, kiwi fruit contains twice as much vitamin C as oranges. Although you can buy ready-made kiwi juice and banana juice, watch out for the sugar content: these delicious fruits are sweet enough, so it's far better to juice your own. To make life easier, you don't even have to peel the kiwis if you've got a half-decent juicer. Natural fruit sugars and the complex carbohydrates in bananas make this an excellent smoothie for instant and slow-release energy. And the colour is simply amazing.

Serves 2
6 kiwi fruit, or 200ml or 7fl oz kiwi juice
4 bananas, or 200ml or 7fl oz
banana juice

1. If using fresh fruit, wash the kiwi fruit and peel the banana. Put them through a juicer, reserving one kiwi fruit.
2. Mix the juices together.
3. Peel and slice the reserved kiwi fruit.
4. Serve the juice with the sliced fruit floating on top.

vital statistics and low carb low-down
Masses of **vitamin C** and a little **vitamin E** from the kiwi fruit, plus its **antioxidant** content of carotenoids, make this a highly **protective** drink. Lots of **potassium** and a little **protein** from the bananas will soon boost your energy levels.

Blackcurrant Tea

low carb rating:

☆ ☆ ☆

You may think it strange to recommend fruit jelly as an energy drink, but it's worth remembering that making jellies is a traditional way of preserving summer fruits to provide nutrients and vitality during the long, cold days of winter. Best of all, make your own with organic fruit, organic sugar, and nothing else. If you're buying it, look for the highest-possible fruit content and products which don't contain colourings, flavourings, and preservatives. Using jelly as a drink – either hot or cold – provides instant benefits, but you can also add it to yoghurts, milk shakes, smoothies or rice pudding.

Serves 2
2 generous tbsp good, organic
   blackcurrant jelly

1. Put the jelly into a large jug.
2. Pour over 500ml or 18fl oz boiling water.
3. Stir well.
4. Cover and leave to cool or serve warm.

vital statistics and low carb low-down

Blackcurrants contain more than four times as much **vitamin C** as oranges and it's in such a stable form that even after freezing, cooking, juicing or turning into jelly or jam, they play a **valuable** role in fighting infection. They contain exceptional amounts of **potassium** but very little sodium, making them **useful** for the treatment of high blood pressure and **fluid retention**. As a hot drink, this recipe is great for **relieving** sore throats, **coughs**, colds, and **general infections**. The pigments that give these currants their colour are some of the most powerful **antioxidants**: they protect against all kinds of cell damage, including cancer. The sugars in this drink are a combination of **fructose** from the blackcurrants, and added **glucose** from the sugars used to make the jelly. Because it's broken down more slowly, fructose doesn't stimulate an instant insulin rush, making this drink much **healthier** than you might think.

Red Alert

low carb rating:

All of the red, yellow, and orange vegetables contain the chemicals your body needs for the replacement of damaged cells. In any illness or at times of excessive stress, overwork, and difficult life situations, your body suffers. This really savoury and delicious juice could make all the difference to your energy levels.

Serves 1–2

1 small red pepper

3 carrots

1 small, fresh uncooked beetroot, preferably with leaves

1 handful of flat-leaf parsley, with stems

1 small handful of watercress leaves

1 Wash and deseed the pepper.
2 Wash the carrots; they don't need peeling, topping or tailing unless they're non-organic.
3 Wash the beetroot and herbs and put all of them, except the watercress, through a juicer.
4 Mix thoroughly and serve with a few watercress leaves on top.

vital statistics and low carb low-down

The red colouring in beetroot is produced by a natural ingredient that **improves** the oxygen-carrying capacity of the **blood** and helps if you're facing extended periods of **physical** and mental exertion. The peppers and carrots are a huge source of **restorative** and **protective** carotenoids and **vitamin C**. Watercress is one of nature's most powerful **cancer-fighters**, with a very specific effect on lung tissue.

Pineapple Bay

low carb rating:

Like all juices, this tastes better and has a higher vitamin and mineral content if you juice it fresh. It will also contain a much larger amount of the enzymes that are so important as a painkiller. To protect these enzymes, make sure that you warm this drink very gently; on no account let it boil.

Serves 2

1 large ripe pineapple, juiced, or 500ml
or 18fl oz pineapple juice
6 bay leaves

1   Put the pineapple juice into a saucepan.
2   Break the bay leaves in half and add to the pan.
3   Heat gently until simmering.
4   Leave for two minutes off the heat.
5   Remove the bay leaves to serve.

vital statistics and low carb low-down

For a **high-energy, low-carb** drink, this one takes some beating. All the energy comes from the natural fruit sugar, **fructose**, which has a much **lower GI** than normal sugar. Although it provides masses of energy, it's much more slowly absorbed through the gut and avoids the peaks and troughs of blood-sugar levels associated with ordinary sugar. **Bromelain** is the natural enzyme in pineapples that accounts for its amazing **therapeutic** properties. This enzyme is specifically **healing** to damaged blood vessels, and speeds the breakdown of clots. For this reason, it's a great **reliever of pain** resulting from trauma and bruising, but it's also one of the most effective natural remedies for all types of sore throats and voice problems. The **essential oils** in bay leaves also help with the pain and discomfort of indigestion.

Strawberry Fair

It may sound like a bit of a fiddle to make, but this juice just oozes energy and vitality. It's no coincidence that grapes are one of the most popular fruits given to sick or convalescing people. They're uniquely nourishing, regenerating, and strengthening. When combined with the protective constituents of peaches, kiwi fruit, and strawberries (not to mention the extraordinary antioxidant powers of passion-fruit and pomegranate), grapes make this is one of the most powerful of all energy juices.

Serves 1–2
6 medium strawberries
175g or 6oz red grapes
2 peaches, stoned
2 unpeeled kiwi fruit
1 pomegranate, seeds and flesh
 scooped out
2 passion fruit, seeds and flesh
 scooped out

1 Wash the strawberries, grapes, peaches, and kiwi fruit, then put all the ingredients through a juicer.
2 Stir in the pomegranate and passion fruit and mix well before serving.

vital statistics and low carb low-down
Rich in **vitamins A** and **C**. Although full of vitamins, this juice is far more valuable for the **tannins, flavones, enzymes,** and other essential **aromatic oils** it provides. Just one glass contains the quintessential **vitality-enhancing** and **life-protecting** elements of Nature. So what are you waiting for? Down the hatch!

Lightly Lychee

low carb rating:

If you've only ever had tinned lychees in syrup in your local Chinese restaurant, this smoothie will be a revelation. Fresh lychees are a totally different taste sensation. They have the most delicate flavour and are also a useful source of nutrients. Using buttermilk rather than yoghurt or ordinary milk provides a different texture as well as an unusual taste to this energy-giving recipe.

Serves 1–2
10 lychees
115ml or 4fl oz buttermilk
3 level tbsp runny honey
2 redcurrant sprigs (for garnish)

1 Peel and stone the lychees. Put the flesh into a blender and whizz.
2 Add the buttermilk and honey and whizz again.
3 Serve with the redcurrants on top.

vital statistics and low carb low-down

Lychees are a good source of **vitamin C**, but they also contain some **calcium**, **potassium**, and **phosphorus**, all of which are important for energy conversion as well as healthy **bones**. The **protein** and extra calcium from the buttermilk, as well as its **extremely low sugar** content, mean you avoid the insulin rush of high-sugar energy-boosters: instead, you **benefit** from a sustained **increase** in your general **vitality**.

Give Us a Pawpaw

low carb rating:

It doesn't matter how good your food is; if it's not digested properly, it's of little benefit – a fact that Shakespeare, with his extraordinary perceptions about the human body and its frailties, knew only too well. "Now, good digestion: wait on appetite, and health to both," says Macbeth in "the Scottish play". The Bard would never have sampled a pawpaw, but he certainly would have approved of this juice, which provides enormous amounts of energy, stimulates the appetite, and improves digestion.

Serves 4
2 large pawpaws, deseeded,
   flesh scooped out of skin
a small bunch of grapes
half a lime, peeled
1 cantaloup melon, peeled

1 Wash the grapes, then put all the ingredients through a juicer.
2 Mix well before serving.

vital statistics and low carb low-down
Super-rich in **vitamins A** and **C** and **betacarotene**. Rich in **potassium**. Contains papain, a **powerful**, protein-digesting **enzyme** that is especially effective on all meats. The tannins in the grape skins are an appetite **stimulant**, while cantaloupe is surprisingly **rich** in nutrients but also contains digestive enzymes. This combination generates **maximum energy** through optimum **digestion**.

American Chai

low carb rating:

Despite its American name, this drink is full of Eastern promise. These spices are used to make traditional American apple pie, but in this tea they supply more than flavour. The tea itself contains healing and protective antioxidants, and all the spices have individual anti-pain properties.

Serves 2
3 cloves
1 cardamom pod
1 stick of cinnamon
2 pinches of ground ginger
1 Darjeeling tea bag
55ml or 2fl oz milk

1 Crush the cloves, cardamom pod, and cinnamon stick using a mortar and pestle.
2 Put into a saucepan and add the ginger and 500ml or 18fl oz water.
3 Bring to a boil, add the tea bag, and leave to rest for five minutes.
4 Add the milk and bring back to a boil.
5 Remove the tea bag, strain, and sweeten to taste.

vital statistics and low carb low-down

In itself, this juice supplies virtually no energy; its secret is the way in which the **spices energize your system** and enable you to up your workload without much effort. The **essential oils** and **phytochemicals** in the spices are the star performers in this drink. Gingerols from the ginger are **warming** and **boost** the **circulation**. The volatile oil cinnamaldehyde from cinnamon is a general tonic and **pain-reliever**. Eugenole from the cloves is the best natural **remedy** for toothache and also **helps** general **aches** and pains. And cardamom is a very specific **heart tonic** in Ayurvedic medicine. This combination will help you through **sustained** and vigorous physical effort – and its **analgesic** benefits will **ease aching muscles** after a heavy weekend's gardening, a tough game of football or tennis, or (if you're mad enough) the rigours of a marathon run.

Easy Peasy

low carb rating:

This is a sort of instant pea soup – and just what's needed for anyone feeling a bit under the weather or suffering from seasonal affective disorder (SAD). Frozen peas are ideal for this delicious and energizing tonic, as they're quick and easy to prepare and lose very little of their nutritional value. Canned peas, on the other hand, lose much more vitamin C and are also generally high in salt. The spring onions and the mint add extra essential oils to boost resistance and energy levels.

Serves 2
1 large spring onion
170g or 6oz frozen peas
1 large sprig of mint, washed
400ml or 14fl oz stock made with
  low-salt commercial cubes or,
  far better, use the recipe for
  Veggie Mug on page 97

1 Wash and trim the spring onions.
2 Mix with the other ingredients and warm gently in a saucepan until the peas are tender.
3 Reserving two tablespoons of peas, liquidize the stock mixture, adding boiling water if necessary.
4 Serve warm with the reserved peas on top.

vital statistics and low carb low-down

Any form of extended stress, anxiety or depression drains the body's energy and vitamin B stores, and fresh or frozen peas are an excellent source of **vitamin B_1**, **folic acid**, **protein**, and **phytochemicals**. They also provide useful quantities of **vitamins A** and **C**, and fatigue-fighting minerals **zinc** and **iron**. Antibacterial and **antiviral** compounds in the onions help **fight infection**, making this an extra-valuable remedy for energy-sapping infections such as flu.

Performance Pears

low carb rating

Never underestimate the power of pears! Few people realize the nutritional value that may be found in a ripe pear of any variety – and the juice adds a unique flavour to this delicious drink. Even just sniffing its wonderful aroma helps set the stage for a real "feel-good" day. If you're feeling a bit sluggish, then the soluble fibre found in the pears and apples, together with the rich supply of natural sugars in grapes and pineapple, are just the thing to aid digestion and provide instant energy.

Serves 2–3

4 unpeeled pears
12 black or white grapes
2 unpeeled apples, uncored
and quartered
2 slices of pineapple, peeled

1 Wash the pears, grapes, and apples, then put all the ingredients through a juicer.
2 Stir well to serve.

vital statistics and low carb low-down

Rich in **potassium**, **pectin** (soluble fibre), and natural healing **enzymes**. Contains **vitamin C**, **calcium**, and traces of **B vitamins**. In addition to its wealth of **vitamins** and **nutrients**, this juice has many other health benefits. The **tannins, powerful flavones,** and other aromatic compounds in grapes combine to make them energizing and **cancer-fighting** – all this in a drink that tastes as great as it smells!

Power Packed

low carb rating:

This is the ultimate energy juice, ideal as a regular booster once or twice a week, and essential at times of greater stress, increased workload or any time when your body and mind need to be bursting with vitality and creative energy. It also promotes greater concentration and is an aid to mental agility and physical activity – definitely power packed.

Serves 2

1 small handful of watercress

1 small handful of spinach

1 kiwi fruit, unpeeled

1 medium tomato

1 large carrot; topped, tailed and peeled unless organic

1 apple, unpeeled but cored and quartered

1 Wash all the ingredients, then put them through a juicer.

2 Mix well before serving.

vital statistics and low carb low-down

Super-rich in **vitamin C**. Rich in **vitamin A**, **betacarotene**, **potassium**, **magnesium**, and **zinc**. Contains **iron**, **calcium**, and **lycopene**. Because of its high vitamin C content – more, in fact, than your minimum daily requirement – this juice will help ward off many a common cold or bout of flu. Its lycopene **guards** against **heart disease** and **cancer** – not bad for something that is also a **terrific energy-booster**.

Green Dream

low carb rating:

Here's another super-energy juice with plenty of essential nutrients and some surprisingly potent natural phytochemicals from the coriander and spinach. It makes an excellent drink for physically active people as it provides a boost of instant energy from the natural sugars in the carrots and kiwi fruit. It is also a good source of potassium – so important for muscle performance.

Serves 1–2
4 carrots
1 kiwi fruit
1 small handful of fresh coriander,
with stems
1 handful of baby spinach leaves

1 Wash all the ingredients. Peel, top and tail the carrots (unless they're organic). Leave the kiwi fruit unpeeled.
2 Put all the ingredients into a juicer, reserving a few coriander leaves.
3 Mix well and serve with coriander leaves on top.

vital statistics and low carb low-down

This **vitality** drink provides a double dose of **betacarotene** and **potassium** from the carrots and kiwi fruit, along with extra **magnesium** and plenty of **vitamin C**. The spinach adds extra **carotenoid**s and a powerful **boost** of **cancer-fighting** plant chemicals. The coriander contains heart- and **circulatory-protective** coumarins and also an effective **antiseptic** essential oil called linalol.

Spice Girl

low carb rating:

This juice contains the powerful volatile oils zingiberene and gingerol in the ginger, as well as the cleansing and digestive benefits of carrot, apple, and orange. This energy juice also has powerful antiseptic and anti-inflammatory benefits and is perfect to use at the onset of a cold or fever, or immediately after a bout of food poisoning.

Serves 1–2

1 apple, unpeeled but cored and quartered

2 carrots; peeled, topped and tailed unless organic

30g or 1oz fresh root ginger, peeled and sliced

1 orange, peeled and pith removed

1   Wash the apple and carrots, then put all the ingredients through a juicer.
2   Stir well to serve.

vital statistics and low carb low-down

Low glycemic index fructose and the **energy-stimulating** properties of ginger make this juice really special. Rich in **vitamins A**, C, and **fibre**, ginger is one of the most versatile and **valuable** of spices. The ancient Greeks used it for **digestive problems** and as an **antidote** to poisoning, while medieval herbalists valued its warming properties highly. In the many ginger recipes you'll find in this book, it also provides an **invigorating energy lift**.

Beet This

low carb rating:

Here is a power-pumping iron tonic in a glass for those dull, grey days when you just can't seem to charge up the batteries. It's all too easy to dismiss the cucumber as nothing more than water. While its nutritional content is very low, it is nonetheless regarded as an important healing vegetable in natural medicine. Here, the cucumber's cool, refreshing flavour contrasts superbly with the astringency of beetroot, spinach, and watercress.

Serves 2
1 small beetroot, unpeeled, with leaves
1 medium cucumber
2 apples, unpeeled but
  cored and quartered
1 small handful of watercress
1 small handful of spinach leaves

1 Wash all the ingredients well, then put them through a juicer.
2 Mix well before serving.

vital statistics and low carb low-down

Super-rich in **iron**, vitamin C, and **folic acid**. Rich in betacarotene and other carotenoids. The **vitamin C** in this juice makes the **iron** it contains all the more easily absorbed by the body, while its **betacarotene** and other **carotenoids** protect against cancers. All this, plus its **instant supply of natural sugars**, makes this the perfect juice for serious exercisers, body-builders, vegetarians, and women planning pregnancy.

Drinks

With

Far too few people drink an adequate volume of liquid – and the little they do drink is often far from healthy. Of course, there's nothing wrong with two or three cups of coffee a day, but nine or ten are bad news. Although modest amounts of coffee make you feel good, and tea is a strong antioxidant which helps protect your heart and blood vessels, excessive amounts of either will give you too much caffeine, which irritates the central nervous system, stops you sleeping, and can leave you feeling agitated. Too much tea can also interfere with the way your body absorbs minerals such as iron and calcium.

And I'm constantly appalled when I see parents who wouldn't dream of giving their six-year-old a double espresso happily allowing them huge quantities of cola, which also contains caffeine. Even if other fizzy drinks don't contain caffeine, many of them include other chemicals which increase the amount of calcium your body excretes – a potential risk for osteoporosis in later life. Everyone knows that two glasses of red wine a day are good for the heart, but make that two bottles and you're heading for serious health (and social) problems.

a Meal

So what do you do if you're trying to be healthy, drink enough to protect your kidneys and prevent urinary infections, avoid the eight teaspoons of sugar in some fizzy drinks, and keep your carbohydrate consumption at sensible levels? The answer is simple: just take the time and trouble to prepare these drinks to enjoy with your meals. Some may look rather strange and include ingredients you wouldn't normally associate with a lunchtime drink or a glass to serve with supper. But, hand on heart, I can tell you they all taste good. What's more, they'll all do you good in a variety of ways.

Dandelion leaves, for example, are a diuretic: especially around period time as they help get rid of excess fluid, reducing the discomfort of swollen feet, ankles, hands, fingers, and breasts. Turmeric, whose unique flavour usually makes us think of spicy food, is a powerful protector against stomach cancer. Marigold petals are antiseptic and antifungal. Ginger relieves travel sickness and early morning sickness in pregnancy. In the following pages, you'll find drinks made with modest amounts of alcohol and low-carb drinks based on – wait for it – *chocolate*.

Bittermint Chocolate

low carb rating:

Here's some delicious chocolate, with the feel-good factor it always brings – and, according to latest research, heart benefits, too. In this recipe, it's combined with mint, which protects you from indigestion, making it particularly useful for anyone who has chronic and long-term digestive problems.

Serves 2

85g or 3oz of organic, good-quality (at least 70 per cent cocoa solids) plain mint chocolate, like Green & Black's

400ml or 14fl oz skimmed milk

4 small sprigs of fresh peppermint, washed

1 Grate about 15g (½ oz) of the chocolate and reserve.
2 Break the rest into chunks and put into a saucepan with the milk and two sprigs of peppermint.
3 Bring slowly to the boil, stirring until the chocolate is dissolved.
4 Fish out the mint.
5 Whisk or froth with a cappuccino wand.
6 Pour into mugs and serve with the grated chocolate and extra mint floating on top.

vital statistics and low carb low-down

Despite the chocolate, this delicious drink is still **low in carbohydrates** because dark chocolate has far **less fat and sugar** than milk varieties. Mint is probably the oldest-known **remedy** for **indigestion** and **stomach acidity** and has been used by herbalists for this reason for centuries. Peppermint oil is still a constituent of many **medicinal digestive** remedies, and taking your mint in this form is strongly protective against many forms of digestive discomfort. Unlike most "after-dinner" mints, you get the **protective benefits** of the best chocolate and the digestive help from the mint with no added sugar or artificial additives whatsoever.

Take a Turn

low carb rating:

Ignore the strange colour; just close your eyes and inhale the tropical aroma of this fantastic concoction. It's best made with cloudy, unfiltered apple juice so that you get the texture and the pectin – a special type of soluble fibre which, as a bonus, helps reduce cholesterol levels. This drink is a great accompaniment to any spicy food.

Serves 2
300ml or 10½fl oz apple juice
4 cloves
½ tsp ground turmeric
1 large sprig of mint, washed

1. Put all the ingredients into a saucepan and warm gently.
2. Allow to rest for five minutes off the heat.
3. To serve, remove the mint, but leave in the cloves as decoration.

vital statistics and low carb low-down

This drink is **highly protective** and has a very **low carbohydrate content**. Eugenol from the cloves is a good general **pain-reliever** and also an effective **antiseptic**. If you have a sore throat, **toothache** or earache, this drink is a good start. The mint will help most types of **digestive** pain, particularly acid **indigestion** and **heartburn**. Turmeric is both **cancer-preventive** and a powerful **anti-inflammatory**, so it helps the pain of arthritis, **rheumatism**, menstrual pains, and other inflammatory problems.

Lemon and Ginger Tea

low carb rating:

I'm not a great lover of the quick fix, especially as this usually means covering up symptoms and sweeping problems under the carpet. But when you're feeling a bit low, run down, and one degree under, here's a quick fix that I really do recommend. Nothing works quite as well as this extremely simple but deliciously stimulating drink. The cleansing citrus flavour of the lemon is an ideal combination with the tropical heat of ginger. Together they provide an almost instant mood-boost, raising energy and gingering up the circulation. This palate-cleansing tonic goes well with any meal.

Serves 2–3
2.5cm or 1 inch fresh ginger root
565ml or 20fl oz boiling water
1 unwaxed lemon

1. Peel and grate the ginger root.
2. Cover with the boiling water.
3. Add the juice of half the lemon and leave to cool.
4. Put in the refrigerator to chill.
5. Strain and serve with slices taken from the other lemon half.

vital statistics and low carb low-down

Lemons provide much more than just **vitamin C**: they're also a rich source of natural **bioflavonoids**, which help **strengthen** and protect the walls of your blood vessels. Add ginger's essential natural oils (gingerols and zingiberine), and you'll **benefit** from centuries of ancient wisdom. Ginger has been used in Chinese medicine for several thousand years and is one of the most effective **stimulants** in the ancient herbal repertoire. Unlike caffeine or alcohol, this drink has **no side-effects** and doesn't leave you feeling even more deflated within the hour.

Prim and Proper

low carb rating:

No, I'm not away with the fairies. There really *are* primrose leaves and flowers in this recipe. Primroses are naturally anti-inflammatory and you can cook the leaves just like spinach (in the water clinging to them after washing), drizzled with extra-virgin olive oil and sprinkled with nutmeg. Make sure you eat the flowers, too: they taste good and also have healing powers. A perfect partner for a healthy lunch, and particularly for anyone with chronically painful problems such as rheumatism or arthritis.

Serves 2

4 carrots, peeled, topped, and tailed unless organic

half a white cabbage

150ml or 5fl oz apple juice

4 primrose leaves, washed and coarsely chopped

2 primrose flowers, washed

1. Put the carrots and cabbage through a juicer, then into a saucepan.
2. Add the apple juice and primrose leaves and bring slowly to a boil.
3. Decorate each mug with a primrose flower.

vital statistics and low carb low-down

The mixture of carrots, cabbage, and apple juice is full of **protective** antioxidants, and even after heating will still provide significant quantities of **vitamin C**. If you have any sort of infection, this juice will help, as it **stimulates** the **immune** system and also contains **antibacterial** sulphur from the cabbage. The **anti-inflammatory** benefits of primrose help with all pains associated with inflammation.

Onion Tea

low carb rating:

This is a bit like quick, clear onion soup. It tastes great (as long as you like onions) and it's extremely therapeutic. Onions have had a revered place in folk medicine for thousands of years and they've been valued equally by Native Americans, Chinese herbalists, and early Middle Eastern physicians. As well as drinking this tea to improve your circulation, if you suffer with chilblains, try rubbing them with a thick wedge of raw onion. This robust drink – a traditional remedy for chest conditions – won't go well with a delicate fish dish, but it is a perfect partner for a hunky beef or vegetable stew.

Serves 2
1 large or 2 small onions
1 tbsp good liquid seasoning,
   like Kallo Organic Vegetable Extract
15g or ½ oz demerara sugar

1   Peel the onion and slice into thin rounds.
2   Put into a saucepan and cover with water (about 400ml or 14fl oz).
3   Add liquid seasoning and sugar.
4   Bring to a boil and simmer for ten minutes.
5   Strain to serve.

vital statistics and low carb low-down

Onions have **mild diuretic** properties, so where fluid retention is linked to raised blood pressure, this tea could be valuable. The strongest **circulatory stimulus** comes from the **enzyme** allinase and from sulphur compounds. The combined effect is a **drop** in **cholesterol** levels, a **reduction** in the **stickiness** of the blood, making it less likely to clot, and an overall **improvement** in **circulation**.

Pink Panther

low carb rating:

Pink is the colour of romance – and a lovingly prepared meal is often the prelude to a quiet night at home *à deux*. Throughout the Middle East, as well as in the England of sixteenth-century herbalist Nicholas Culpepper, the aroma, taste, and texture of roses have been used to heighten feelings of love and romance. That's just what this light and lovely drink can do for you.

Serves 2
2 pink grapefruit*
85ml or 3fl oz rose water
rose petals for garnish

***If taking prescribed medicines, consult your doctor before drinking large amounts of grapefruit juice.**

1 Juice the grapefruit.
2 Heat the juice gently in a saucepan.
3 Pour into two cups or heatproof glasses.
4 Divide the rose water between the glasses and stir briefly.
5 Scatter the rose petals on top to serve.

vital statistics and low carb low-down

Using pink grapefruit for this drink matters: they're not only **sweeter** than the paler varieties, but also **enhance** the deepness of the colour. Rose petals – or rose-hips if you can't get them – contain **mood-enhancing essential oils**, which are also thought to be an **aphrodisiac**. Diluted rose-hip syrup is a suitable substitute if you can't find rose water.

Clean-Up Juice

This packed-with-goodness juice is full of spring and summer flavours, filled with vitamins. It's an excellent way to stimulate a sluggish system with blood-purifying and body-cleansing nutrients and makes a wonderful complement to any Mediterranean-style meal. If you're trying to lose weight, you can use it as a meal replacement. Just look at its vital statistics!

Serves 2–3
1 large handful of spinach leaves
1 large handful of watercress
¼ red pepper, deseeded
half a medium cucumber
1 large leaf of spring greens
**3 carrots, peeled, topped, and tailed
   unless organic**

1   Wash all the ingredients then put them through a juicer.
2   Stir well to serve.

vital statistics and low carb low-down
Super-rich in **vitamin A** and **carotenoids**. Rich in **sulphur** and **vitamin C**. This juice is more important for its **phytochemicals** than basic vitamins and minerals. Special carotenoids in spinach and spring greens **protect** the **eyes** against degenerative diseases, and the extra betacarotenes from red pepper and cucumber help **revitalize** skin and the mucous membranes of the nose and throat. A great **boost** for the **immune system** and for increased **vitality,** and has **hardly a carb** in sight.

Carrot Cup

low carb rating:

Delicious as a drink on its own, this juice is also a good accompaniment to meat dishes because the enzymes in pineapple help promote healthy digestion. The healing properties of the carrots combine well with the soothing effect of cucumber on the mucous membranes, and the diuretic action of celery reduces swelling of the tonsils, adenoids, and throat. Add sage, which is powerfully antiseptic and a traditional remedy for all mouth and throat problems, and you have real ammunition against common year-round health complaints.

Serves 3–4

3 unpeeled carrots; unless organic, remove top and bottom

1 small pineapple, peeled

3 celery sticks, with leaves

half a large cucumber

6 fresh sage leaves

1. Wash all the ingredients then put them through a juicer.
2. Mix well before serving.

vital statistics and low carb low-down

Super-rich in **betacarotene**, **potassium**, and natural **enzymes**. Contains **vitamin C** and **folic acid**. The natural enzyme **bromelain** in pineapple is especially **healing** to the lining of the mouth and throat; it's also a great aid to **digestion**, so it maximizes the extraction of **nutrients** from foods. Sage is a valuable **antiseptic** due to its high content of the **essential oil** known as thujone. All this and **low carbs** too!

Pack a Punch

low carb rating:

This is a great pre-barbecue ice-breaker to be sipped gently under the shade of a large garden umbrella. But who needs an excuse to enjoy any form of Pimm's? It's cool, refreshing, and, in moderation, extremely good for your health. You'll love the interesting mixture of Pimm's and the sweet tartness of good pink grapefruit. This punch will certainly cool you down on a hot day – even when it's grey, wet, and miserable, it will cheer you up with its wonderful suggestion of smooth, green lawns and summer sunshine.

For 10 party-loving people
4 pink grapefruit*
ice cubes
half a 375ml bottle of Pimm's
half a bottle of good sparkling wine
1 litre or 35fl oz fizzy mineral water
1 unwaxed lemon

*If taking prescribed medicines, consult your doctor before drinking large amounts of grapefruit juice.

1. Squeeze the juice from the grapefruit using a citrus-fruit or hand-held juicer (DON'T put them through a juicing machine made for harder fruits).
2. Put some ice into a large punch-bowl.
3. Pour the juice, Pimm's, and sparkling wine over the ice.
4. Stir well, then top up with the mineral water.
5. Slice the lemon thinly and use it as a garnish.

vital statistics and low carb low-down

Nobody goes to a barbecue for a totally carb-free experience: in any case, **no-carb diets** are **unbalanced, unhealthy, and potentially dangerous.** You don't need an excuse to enjoy the modest amount of alcohol in this drink. Pink grapefruit provides abundant amounts of **vitamin C** and also some **betacarotene.** Grapefruit contains **bioflavonoids,** too, which play an important part in **protecting** the inside walls of veins and arteries. Though red wine is reputedly the heart-protector, all alcoholic drinks are **good** for your heart and **circulation** as long as you don't drink too much.

French Connection

low carb rating:

So what *is* the connection between the French and a drink based on prunes? It's because the best prunes in the world come from the small French town of Agen, where they've been grown for more than 800 years. *Pruneaux d'Agen* on the package means the same as *appellation contrôlée* on a bottle of fine wine. Californian prunes, however, are far more widely available, less expensive, and equally nutritious. Prunes are famed for their gentle laxative action, but because of their high potassium content, they're good for high blood pressure, too. This is the perfect accompaniment to Sunday brunch, because its robust flavours are wonderful with eggs, cured meats, and any type of sausage or salami. It's age-defying, cancer-beating, heart-protective, and even helps prevent wrinkles.

Serves 2–3

4 apples, unpeeled, uncored, and quartered

4 pears, unpeeled

6 prunes, soaked and stoned

1 dessertspoon lecithin granules

1 dessertspoon molasses

1. Wash and juice the apples and pears.
2. Purée the prunes in a blender.
3. Add the apple and pear juice to the prunes and whizz until combined.
4. Spoon in the lecithin and molasses and blitz again.

vital statistics and low carb low-down

This drink has a moderate carbohydrate content, but is **high in antioxidants**. Super-rich in **vitamin C**, rich in **potassium**, and contains **vitamin E**. This juice has a wide range of **health benefits**. It's good for **digestion** and constipation, and ideal for those suffering from arthritis, rheumatism or gout. The **lecithin** helps improve **brain function** and **memory**, and the extra **iron** and **potassium** from molasses, together with the enormous amount of soluble **fibre** from the apples and pears, **lower** cholesterol, **reduce** blood pressure, and **protect** the heart.

Lemon and Angostura Tonic

low carb rating:

Pink G&T – without the gin! Both pink gin and gin and tonic were favourites among the British Empire colonials living in India at the time of the Raj. I've never been sure why they enjoyed this drink so much or whether it was the tonic water or bitters that simply disguised how much alcohol they were actually consuming. You'll be amazed how soothing it tastes when warm.

Serves 2
2 unwaxed lemons
400ml or 14fl oz tonic water
4 shakes Angostura bitters

1 Juice the lemons and cut off two slices of rind.
2 Mix together the juice and tonic water and warm gently.
3 Add the Angostura and reserved lemon rind to serve.

vital statistics and low carb low-down
This **ultra-low carbohydrate** drink goes brilliantly with spicy dishes that feature curries or chillies. The most important ingredient in tonic water is **quinine**, one of the earliest known of all **anti-malarial** preparations and made from the bark of the rain forest **cinchona** tree. The myth tells how a young man with malaria drank from a pool into which the tree had fallen and lain for years. Within hours, the man's terrible fever had passed and the discovery was made. The result is true, even if the story isn't, but the **pain relief** comes from quinine's power to **prevent cramp**. The lemons, of course, provide extra **vitamin C**.

Real Lemon Barley Water

low carb rating:

No summer tea party should be without this refreshing English favourite, but lemon barley water has been a traditional cleansing formula of herbalists for hundreds of years. It is particularly effective for all forms of urinary problems, and a great cleansing aid for most skin conditions, particularly those associated with oily skin. Any of the three herbs enhance the cleansing abilities of this drink, and the high-fibre content of the barley means that one glass can provide up to a third of your daily fibre needs, making this an excellent bowel cleanser as well. Try it and it will become one of your family favourites; the kids, particularly, will love it.

Serves 4
125g or 4½ oz pot barley
55g or 2oz organic demerara sugar
2 unwaxed lemons
1.2 litres or 42fl oz water
a handful of marigold petals, dandelion
   leaves or marjoram
ice cubes

1 Wash the barley and put it into a large jug.
2 Put the sugar into a bowl. Scrub the lemons with warm water and grate the rind into the sugar. Mix together and add to the barley.
3 Bring the water to the boil, pour over the barley, sugar, and lemon rind. Stir vigorously and leave to cool.
4 Squeeze the juice from the lemons, add to the barley, stir again, and strain through a fine sieve. If you have access to marigold petals, dandelion leaves or fresh marjoram, they make an unusual addition: if not, buy marjoram.
5 Serve over lots of ice cubes.

vital statistics and low carb low-down

The naturally **cleansing** plant chemicals in marigolds, dandelions, and marjoram are what give this drink its real **boost**, though the very high **vitamin C** content is a major cleansing factor, too. Because of the lemon peel, there's also a rich content of **bioflavonoids**, which are cleansing and **protective**. As well as the **fibre** from the barley, there are modest amounts of **B vitamins**, some **trace minerals**, and a small amount of **protein**. This traditional beverage is free from all artificial colourings, flavourings, and preservatives.

Parsley, Sage, Rosemary, and . . .

low carb rating:

Just like the traditional folk-song made famous by Simon and Garfunkel, this juice is the ideal combination of vitality and calming influences. It is a low-carbohydrate drink that goes particularly well with salads and vegetable dishes, as well as being good for the body, mind, and spirit. It also enhances memory, is cleansing, and – thanks to the sage and thyme – is mildly antiseptic.

Serves 3–4
1 handful of parsley, with stalks
6 sage leaves
2 tsp rosemary leaves, removed
   from stalks
the leaves from 1 small sprig of thyme
4 carrots, peeled, topped, and tailed
   unless organic
3 celery sticks, with leaves

1 Wash all the ingredients and put them through a juicer.
2 Mix thoroughly before serving.

vital statistics and low carb low-down

Super-rich in **vitamin A** and **carotenoids**. Rich in **vitamin C** and **folic acid**. Contains **potassium**, **calcium**, and small amounts of other **B vitamins**. The natural **diuretic** properties of celery and parsley give this drink enormous **cleansing** properties, while the sage **stimulates** liver function, the rosemary improves **memory** and **concentration**, and the thyme is a good **antiseptic**. An excellent all-round healthy herbal drink.

Sting in the Tail

low carb rating:

Be sure to wear gloves when gathering the stinging nettles, but don't worry – the juice won't sting. Nettles have been used as medicine since the earliest times and were one of the favourite herbs of the first-century Greek physician Dioscorides. This powerful herb, combined with the immune-boosting benefits of carrots and spinach, makes this an instant tonic.

Serves 2–3

1 bunch of young, pale-green stinging nettles

2 cooking apples – ideally Bramleys – unpeeled, uncored, and quartered

3 carrots, peeled, topped, and tailed unless organic

1 handful of spinach leaves

1 Wash all the ingredients well, then put them through a juicer.
2 Stir well to serve.

vital statistics and low carb low-down

As cooking apples contain less sugar than dessert varieties, this drink gives you all their benefits with far **fewer carbohydrates**. It's the ideal addition to a lunchbox – no matter how old the "child". Super-rich in **vitamin A**. Rich in **vitamin C**. Contains **calcium**, **potassium**, and **iron**. The **flavonoids** in spinach and nettles boost this drink's **protective** value, while the vitamin C from the apples improves **absorption** of its **iron** content. This is an ideal juice for nursing mothers as it increases the flow of breast milk, guards against **anaemia**, and **restores energy**.

Be

Everyone will have the occasional bad night's sleep. Stress, anxiety, pain, indigestion, strange beds, a snoring partner, or even the weather can be to blame. But for the chronic insomniac, life can be extremely difficult. Sadly, this has become such a common problem that fatigue, exhaustion, and poor sleep are among the most frequent causes of visits to the doctor. The worst thing you can do about insomnia is to work yourself up into state of anger, frustration, depression or anxiety: any of these emotions will just make matters worse. Start by looking at the practical things. As an osteopath, I'm always horrified by the number of patients I see who suffer from both backache and insomnia. They've been married twenty years, owned six cars, three TVs, five vacuum cleaners, and four lawnmowers, but they're still sleeping in the same bed they bought when they got married. Dieting and sleep don't go well together, either. Going to bed hungry is guaranteed to bring on a restless night. Conversely, a huge meal very late in the evening can result in heartburn and indigestion, which won't help much. Limping through life on a crutch of sleeping pills isn't the answer, nor is alcohol. While both may

time

Drinks

induce sleep, it's the wrong type of sleep. It makes you miss out on the refreshing dream stages, so you wake in the morning feeling hungover, headachy, and horrible. Sleep hygiene should be your first line of attack. That means getting yourself into regular habits. Set the alarm for the same time every morning, whether you have to get up or not, and try going to bed as close to the same time every night. Try using some of the simple and non-habituating herbal remedies such as valerian, hops, or passiflora. Add essential oils of lavender, camomile, and rose to a warm bedtime bath. It's also worth taking up some form of yoga, meditation or relaxation exercise. A soothing massage can often work wonders – and this is a really easy DIY treatment with the aid of a good book and lots of practice. And of course, one of the best remedies of all is sex. Whatever you choose, you have to make a determined effort – and there couldn't be a simpler starting point than the delicious recipes in this chapter. None of them will knock you out like a zombie or leave you feeling muddle-headed in the morning. What they will do is help you unwind, relax, get rid of anxiety, and prepare your body physically and mentally for the night ahead.

Beetroot and Celery Booster

low carb rating:

The ribald description of celery is that, as far as men are concerned, it "puts lead in your pencil". That owes more to the ancient herbalists' Doctrine of Signatures – by which the medicinal properties of plants were determined by their physical appearance – than it does to science. The addition of beetroot juice, however, has been scientifically proven to make this a powerful blood-boosting tonic.

Serves 2

4 celery sticks, with leaves if possible

255ml or 9fl oz home-juiced beetroot juice from 4 large beetroot (or a good commercial brand)

1 small handful of flat-leaf parsley

1   Wash and put the celery through a juicer.
2   Strain if it looks too stringy.
3   If making your own beetroot juice, put the beetroot through a juicer.
4   Mix the juices together.
5   Pull the leaves off the parsley stalks, wash, chop finely, and scatter on top.

Note This juice can also be served warm. Scatter the parsley leaves on top after pouring into mugs or heatproof glasses.

vital statistics and low carb low-down

The **essential oils** in celery help to **calm** the nerves and **relax** the mind – an ideal combination for the anxious **insomniac**. The history of beetroot as medicine is documented as far back as the ancient Greeks. Its main benefit is that it is a **powerful blood purifier**. Thanks to the way it **increases** the oxygen-carrying **capacity** of blood, it's also a very effective **tonic**. Celery juice contains **virtually no carbs**, but the beetroot juice has quite a high natural sugar content.

Garlic Nightcap

low carb rating:

It's the salad leaves in this recipe that help banish insomnia, as they contain small traces of an opium-like soporific substance. The whole drink is soothing and helps relieve anxiety – one of the most common bedfellows of sleeplessness.

Serves 1
350g or 12oz mixed salad leaves
1 unwaxed lime, with peel
1 garlic clove, peeled
2 carrots, peeled, topped, and tailed
** unless organic**

1 Wash the salad leaves and the lime.
2 Put all the ingredients through a juicer.
3 Mix well before serving.

vital statistics and low carb low-down
Rich in **vitamins A, C,** and **E.** Contains **chlorophyll, magnesium, potassium,** and **silicon.** As a bonus, Garlic Nightcap contains substances that are essential for **healthy hair.** Enjoy the **calming** natural opiates in the lettuce, the sulphur compounds in the garlic, and the **bioflavonoids** in the lime that **strengthen** the **circulatory system.** It's enough to give anyone a good night's **sleep.**

Barley Broth

low carb rating:

Nothing like the apology for barley water you can buy as a cordial, this is the real McCoy. A traditional sick-room favourite for urinary infections such as cystitis, it's also a great aid to a good night's sleep – and doubly valuable because, as well as helping you gently into the land of nod, it prevents the frequent night-time trips to the bathroom if you have cystitis.

Serves 4
55g or 2oz pot barley
1 large unwaxed lemon
1 large tbsp honey

1 Put the barley into a saucepan and add 850ml or 30fl oz of water.
2 Cut the lemon into thin slices and add to the pot.
3 Simmer for ninety minutes.
4 Strain, stir in the honey, and pour into cups to serve.

vital statistics and low carb low-down

Barley is a very neglected grain. It is broken down into sugars very slowly during digestion. Consequently, it has a **low GI**, making it an excellent low-carb food. It's also a good source of **calcium**, **potassium**, and **B vitamins**. This most ancient of all cultivated cereals has valuable amounts of **fibre**, too and, like all starches, helps trigger the **release** of the natural **sleep-inducing** chemical **tryptophan** in the brain. Honey is widely used in folk medicine as a **sleep promoter** and combines perfectly with the other ingredients to make this a most **pleasant** drink.

Parsley and Ginseng Gusto

low carb rating:

Despite its reputation as a stimulant, the small quantity of ginseng in this drink helps to keep your metabolism ticking over nicely while you sleep, encouraging it to burn off some of those excess calories left over from the day. This may not be the most fragrant or delicately flavoured tea, but it reaches the parts that others teas never reach. The traditional effects of ginseng, the minerals from molasses, and the ancient medicinal history of parsley make this a recipe you'll return to often once you've tried it.

Serves 2
4 heaped tsp fresh parsley, washed and chopped (or 2 tsp dried)
1 tsp liquid ginseng extract
2 tsp molasses

1 Put the parsley into a clean teapot.
2 Pour on 500ml or 18fl oz boiling water.
3 Leave to stand for ten minutes.
4 Strain and pour into mugs.
5 Add the ginseng extract according to packet instructions.
6 Stir in the molasses to taste.

vital statistics and low carb low-down

The **high potassium** content of parsley has effective **calming** properties which will help your body perform its **cleansing**, **growth**, and **repair** functions during the night. Potassium also helps **prevent cramp** – a common cause of painfully disrupted sleep. It's also a good source of **vitamin C** and **iron**. Ginseng, traditionally known as "man root", has been used as an **aphrodisiac** by Chinese physicians for at least 5,000 years, so it could help get your night off to a romantic and **relaxing** start. The **tiny amount of raw sugar** in the molasses is insignificant.

Lavender Cream

low carb rating:

Mention lavender and most people's thoughts turn to little bags of dried flowers or lavender water used by their grannies. Consequently, they find the idea of using lavender in food rather strange. In fact, it's a culinary practice that goes back thousands of years. As well as using it in fragrant drinks like this, you can add it to biscuits, cakes, and ice cream.

Serves 1
140ml or 5fl oz semi-skimmed milk
55ml or 2fl oz full-fat cream
2 lavender stalks with flowers

1 Pour the milk and cream into a saucepan.
2 Add the washed lavender.
3 Gently bring just to the boil.
4 Fish out the lavender.
5 Sieve if necessary before serving.

vital statistics and low carb low-down

The **essential oils** in lavender are renowned for the dramatic way in which they can be used to **relieve headaches**. But lavender is also an effective **antiseptic** and a wonderful **tonic** for the central nervous system. For anyone whose vitality has been badly affected by stress, anxiety or depression – which often destroy sleep – this **rich** and indulgent drink is a true **elixir**. Lavender is also one of the most effective **sleep-inducing** herbs; just smelling the fragrance is a helpful **aid** if you find getting to sleep a problem.

Veggie Mug

low carb rating:

If you think warm milk is a good bedtime drink, just wait until you try this one. I know it sounds like a soup, but then what is soup if it isn't a hot drink? What you're actually getting here is a clear, nourishing, and calming bouillon and also the basic recipe for great vegetable stock. Once you've made it, you won't want those horrible, salty stock cubes. It's perfect for freezing as ice cubes, so you can easily defrost however many you need to make an instant hot drink.

Serves 6

1 large carrot; peeled, topped, and tailed unless organic

1 large onion, quartered, with the skin left on

1 turnip, washed and quartered

1 leek, including the green top, thoroughly washed

3 sprigs of mint

6 large stems of parsley

1 Put all the ingredients into a large stockpot.
2 Add 850ml (30fl oz) of water.
3 Bring to a boil, then simmer for one hour.
4 Strain off the vegetables to serve.

vital statistics and low carb low-down

Ultra-low in carbs, this certainly counts as one of your five portions of fruit or veg a day and has a wide range of **health benefits**. Leeks provide **antibacterial** and **antifungal** protection and help ward off chest infections. **Betacarotene** from the carrots is good for the eyes. Parsley helps get rid of excessive fluid, and the fresh mint brings **instant relief** from **indigestion**. The ideal nightcap if you're getting over flu or any other acute **infection**.

Camomile with Lime Blossom

low carb rating:

Camomile and lime blossom … you'd be hard-pressed to think of a more potent double dose of natural sleep-inducing plants. As far as herbalists are concerned, this has to be the absolute dream team, and it's safe and effective for all ages. This is a particularly good drink for children kept awake by headaches, fevers, coughs, colds, and general restlessness. The lime and honey make it taste far better than camomile on its own.

Serves 1
½ tsp dried camomile
½ tsp dried lime blossom
2 tsp lime-blossom honey

1 Put the camomile and lime blossom into a mug or infuser.
2 Pour over 255ml or 9fl oz boiling water.
3 Cover and leave for five minutes.
4 Strain into a clean mug.
5 Sweeten to taste with the honey.

vital statistics and low carb low-down

Camomile has been widely used since herbalists planted it in Queen Elizabeth I's gardens. Its main ingredient is **chamazulene**, which isn't only effective for **reducing temperatures**, but also an extremely good **treatment** for **insomnia**. Lime blossom was a favourite of European herbalists and even now is served as a tisane in fashionable tea and coffee shops.

Lettuce Sleep

low carb rating:

Just the juice to revive that sinking feeling! Of all the lettuces, iceberg probably has the least amount of nutrients – especially when compared with the dark-green and red-leafed varieties. However, it doesn't go slimy in your refrigerator after three days: in fact, it will keep well for up to two weeks if wrapped in clingfilm. It has a much sweeter flavour than other lettuces and contains the highest levels of natural calming substances. If you're tense, anxious, and irritable, as well as run down, this is the cure.

Serves 2–3
half an iceberg lettuce
3 apples, unpeeled, uncored,
and quartered
1 unwaxed lemon, with peel if thin-
skinned

1 Wash and put all the ingredients through a juicer.
2 Mix well before serving.

vital statistics and low carb low-down

Super-rich in **vitamin C** and **folic acid**, with **vitamin A**, **iron**, **calcium**, and masses of **potassium**, this juice is also a good source of **protective flavonoids**. Lettuce contains substances known as **lactones**, and was used by the ancient Assyrians as a mild **sedative**. All of which makes this an ideal **calming** and **restorative** juice – especially for children who are recovering from illness.

Yoghurt Mint

low carb rating:

I don't expect many of you would think of yoghurt as a particularly relaxing ingredient: nor, for that matter, would you expect mint to have soothing properties. The most commonly used mint – peppermint – has a sharp, astringent, and stimulating aroma. But warm these two together and you'll find a delicious, nutritious, and gently relaxing drink.

Serves 1
140ml or 5fl oz live, runny yoghurt
100ml or 3½ fl oz semi-skimmed milk
3 sprigs of fresh mint, preferably
  peppermint, plus 2 leaves for garnish

1 Put the yoghurt, milk, and mint sprigs into a saucepan.
2 Heat very gently for ten minutes.
3 Scoop out the mint.
4 Pour into a mug and serve with the mint leaves on top.

vital statistics and low carb low-down

The milk and yoghurt provide **calcium**, which is naturally **relaxing** and also **stimulates** the brain's release of mood-calming **tryptophan**. The main ingredients of mint are **menthol** and **menthone**, and as well as being one of the best remedies for **digestive problems**, these natural plant chemicals are very relaxing. In addition to a good night's sleep, you'll also be getting a real **bone-building bonus** from the calcium in the dairy products.

Basil Tea

low carb rating:

Herbal teas – or tisanes as they're also known – are the simplest and most effective way of using the medicinal properties of teas at home. They've been used for many thousands of years and can be extremely beneficial for the relief of many health problems. Here, we're using basil, one of the most popular, delicious, and aromatic herbs, which is known throughout the Mediterranean for its calming and soporific properties.

Serves 1

2 heaped tsp of torn fresh basil leaves

OR

1 heaped tsp of dried basil

1 Put the herbs into a mug or *tisanière* (infuser).
2 Pour over about 200ml or 7fl oz boiling water.
3 Cover and allow to sit for about ten minutes.
4 Strain before serving.

vital statistics and low carb low-down

There are many varieties of this attractive, easily grown herb and they all have basically the same **health benefits**. They contain several **volatile oils**, a fair amount of **betacarotene**, and some **vitamin C**. As well as being very relaxing, basil is **cleansing**, **antibacterial**, and **useful** for the **relief** of **kidney** and urinary **problems**.

Sleeping Salad

A large meal too late at night is one of the most common reasons for insomnia. Heartburn, indigestion, wind, and a rumbling stomach aren't exactly conducive to a good eight hours of undisturbed sleep. Forewarned is forearmed, so if you know you're going out for a big meal or a festive function, make sure you have the ingredients to hand so that you can make this drink before you go to bed.

Serves 2–3

1 Little Gem lettuce

500ml or 18fl oz vegetable stock; use the recipe for Veggie Cup (see page 97) or use a good, low-salt, organic cube, such as Kallo

1 tsp fennel seeds

1 Wash the lettuce and shred finely.
2 Put into a saucepan with the stock.
3 Bring to a boil and simmer for five minutes.
4 Meanwhile, crush the fennel seeds finely.
5 Add to the pan and simmer for two more minutes.
6 Sieve to remove any large pieces of lettuce.
7 Serve warm.

vital statistics and low carb low-down

Fennel seeds are an almost magical **cure** for most **gastric disturbances**, and if you think they taste familiar, they're one of the ingredients in **colic treatments** for babies. You're probably surprised to see lettuce in this bedtime cocktail, but **extracts** of the sticky sap in lettuce stalks were used in classical times for the very purpose of **inducing sleep**. They used wild lettuce, which contains a morphine-like substance still present in modern varieties but in smaller quantities.

Mellow Yellow

low carb rating:

Here's a sleep-inducing smoothie that's simply bursting with nutritional value. Lots of protein, minerals, plant hormones, and all the digestive protection of honey are present in this mixture. The saffron adds a wonderful colour, but it's also a mood-enhancer and helps improve digestion. Throughout Asia, most women have a daily intake of some form of soya protein, and it is this component of their diets that is believed to protect them against heart disease, osteoporosis, hot flushes, and the other unpleasant symptoms of the menopause in later life.

Serves 1–2
450ml or 16fl oz soya milk
2 heaped tbsp runny honey
1 large pinch of saffron
1 tbsp ground almonds
1 tsp slivered lightly-roasted almonds

1 Put the first four ingredients into a blender.
2 Whizz until smooth.
3 Serve in glasses with the slivered almonds floating on top.

vital statistics and low carb low-down

Saffron contains the natural ingredients **saffronal**, **cinelle**, and **crocins** and is known to have **antidepressant** and **mood-enhancing** properties. Its main **cleansing** attribute helps to induce menstruation, thus preventing the build-up of waste products. The **phytoestrogens** in soya milk have a weak **hormonal effect** that is especially **beneficial** to women. Although soya extracts are now available as tablets, it's far better to get these substances from food than from pills. Although almonds are quite high in oils and calories, they contain only small amounts of carbohydrate. Like all nuts, almonds are a rich source of **vitamin E**, **essential fatty acids**, and **minerals**.

It is no accident that the practice of medicine is known as "the healing arts". Medicine *is* an art – and its purpose is healing. In our modern, high-tech, science-led world, it's all too easy to forget that the roots and historical origins of healing came originally from the kitchen. Our ancient forebears knew about the healing art of kitchen medicine, which was always the preserve of the tribal medicine man, the village wise woman, or priests, monks, and other religious figures. The history of herbal medicine drew on this huge body of knowledge and refined kitchen recipes into more exact prescriptions. As recently as the early twentieth century, herbalists flourished, the vast majority of doctors' prescriptions were based on natural plants, and every mother knew the basics of the

ealing

Drinks

healing art of kitchen medicine. Then came the pharmaceutical revolution
and the long, slow demise of the role of herbs in everyday treatment.
But now, in the early years of the twenty-first century, when computers
run everything and technology is king, the wheel has come full circle and
plants are once again playing a key role in the development of the latest
treatments for everything from arthritis to cancer. In this chapter, you'll
discover the healing powers of many simple ingredients – fruits,
vegetables, plants, and flowers – that you'll find in almost every kitchen
and garden. Whether you've got a headache or a hangover, flatulence or
flu, water retention or wrinkles, you'll find a simple, pleasant, and effective
answer, and every one a super low-carb drink.

Hopalong

low carb rating:

Hops have been used as a vegetable since Roman times, but they weren't part of the beer-making process until the Middle Ages. Although mostly regarded as a mild sedative and used for centuries for stuffing pillows to help children and adults get a better night's sleep, they have many other properties that warrant their inclusion in this section. If you've got the space to grow this highly decorative plant yourself (they do well in a pot), you can cook the young shoots just like asparagus, as they make an excellent iron-rich early summer tonic.

Serves 1
1 tbsp dried hops (or 1 hop tea bag)
1 tsp maple syrup

1. If using an infuser, put the hops into the central compartment, pour in about 255ml or 9fl oz boiling water, cover, and leave for five minutes.
2. If using commercial hop tea bags, make the tea in a mug, following the instructions on the packet.
3. Remove the centre of the infuser or take out the tea bag.
4. Sweeten with maple syrup to serve.

vital statistics and low carb low-down

One common cause of **fatigue** and constant **exhaustion** is the poor absorption of nutrients due to faulty digestion. The **essential oils** in hops both **stimulate** the **appetite** and **improve** the **digestive process** so that by eating better and extracting maximum nutritional value from your meals, you'll **restore** your **vitality**.

Egg Tea

low carb rating:

This is egg nog with a difference: there's no alcohol. Because you're using a raw egg yolk in this recipe, do be sure to buy organic and certified salmonella-free eggs. Even so, this is not suitable in pregnancy or for anyone whose immune system may be compromised by medication or serious illness. The mild stimulus of the tea and the super nutrition in the egg yolk are what made this a real sick-room favourite of the Victorians.

Serves 1
1 egg
Darjeeling tea or tea bag
  (enough for one person)
sugar to taste

1 Separate the egg and discard the white.
2 Beat the yolk until creamy.
3 Make the tea according to packet instructions.
4 Put the yolk into a mug, then pour the tea on top.
5 Stir well and sweeten with sugar to taste.

vital statistics and low carb low-down

If you're feeling unwell, eating and drinking can seem like a chore, so it's important that what little food you do consume is crammed full of good **nutrition**. Egg yolk is the richest natural source of **lecithin**, which is vital for many of the body's **metabolic** processes. It **protects** against heart disease and makes it easier for the body to convert fats into much-needed **energy**. The benefits of the **vitamins** and **minerals** are enhanced by the mild stimulus from the caffeine in tea. Tea is also a rich source of **immune**-boosting antioxidants.

Super Celery

low carb rating:

From a strictly nutritional standpoint, celery is a pretty poor source of vitamins and minerals, although it does contain some folic acid and potassium. If you have the unblanched, green celery and you also eat the leaves, you'll get a modest amount of betacarotene, too.

Serves 2
2 large heads of celery, with the leafy tops
1 tsp crushed celery seeds

1 Cut off the celery tops, reserving two sprigs, and the outer stalks. (Keep the hearts to use in salads or as a braised vegetable.)
2 Slice the tops and outer stalks, and put them with the seeds into a medium saucepan.
3 Cover with 600ml or 20fl oz of water.
4 Bring to the boil and simmer for one hour.
5 Strain into heatproof glasses and serve with the reserved celery sprigs floating on top.

vital statistics and low carb low-down

Much prized by the Roman physicians and equally popular with eighteenth-century European herbalists, celery is a **gentle** but mild and **natural diuretic** and a **treatment** for kidney and urinary **infections**. The major **healing** properties come from its **essential oils**, which combine to make celery **soothing**, **calming**, and excellent for the **relief** of **anxiety**. And yes, it's probably true that you **use more calories chewing** it than you consume by eating it: that's why it's every slimmer's friend. You might also be surprised to know that other substances in both the seeds and the rest of the plant give it the reputation of being a **gentle aphrodisiac**. That can't be bad for a low-carb, healing drink!

Lemon Verbena Tea

low carb rating:

Without doubt, lemon verbena is a plant that amply repays the trouble of growing it yourself. It will do well in a large pot or in the ground, but it isn't hardy and pots need to be taken into a greenhouse or conservatory in winter. It will grow anything up to ten feet high with an eight-feet spread, but if left in the soil, it needs a sheltered position and you must mulch all around the roots to protect it from frost. It's the best of all lemon-scented plants, and its leaves are easy to dry.

Serves 1

2 tsp chopped fresh lemon verbena or 1 commercial tea bag

2 drops vanilla essence

1 If using the fresh herb, put into a cup or infuser.
2 Pour in 255ml or 9fl oz freshly boiled water.
3 Cover, rest for ten minutes, and strain.
4 If using a tea bag, follow the packet instructions, then take out the tea bag.
5 Stir in the vanilla essence to serve.

vital statistics and low carb low-down

This South American plant has a long history among herbalists as a **gentle sedative**. A rich source of the essential oils **limonene** and **geraniolle**, lemon verbena is a valuable **antidepressant**. If you do have your own plant, the leaves, fresh or dried, add a unique flavour to cooked fruits or ice cream, and they'll provide you with this year-round **low-carb** tea and an endless source of potpourri fragrances.

Grapes with Celery

low carb rating:

To most people, celery is something to eat with a piece of cheese or add to a tasty dip for quail eggs or radishes. And very delicious these dishes are, too. One thing many people don't know, however, is that celery is a useful diuretic, one of the most powerful natural medicines known to fight fluid retention. Its medicinal benefits have been used in herbal medicine for thousands of years.

Serves 2
1 tbsp crushed celery seed
300ml or 10½fl oz white grape juice
**4 small, white, seedless,
   fine-skinned grapes**

1   Using a pestle and mortar, crush the celery seed until very fine.
2   Put into a saucepan with the grape juice.
3   Heat gently and pour into heatproof glasses.
4   Wash and halve the grapes and serve with them floating in each glass.

vital statistics and low carb low-down
More than 5,000 years ago, Chinese herbalists preceded Hippocrates in their use of celery seeds as a **calming remedy**. They're **stress-relieving**, and whether eaten with food or used ground in drinks (as here), they're extremely effective. Grapes are exceptionally **nourishing** and **sustaining**. This makes them a valuable **healing** food after long periods of stress and anxiety. As a bonus, they're one of the most **cancer-fighting** of all fruits.

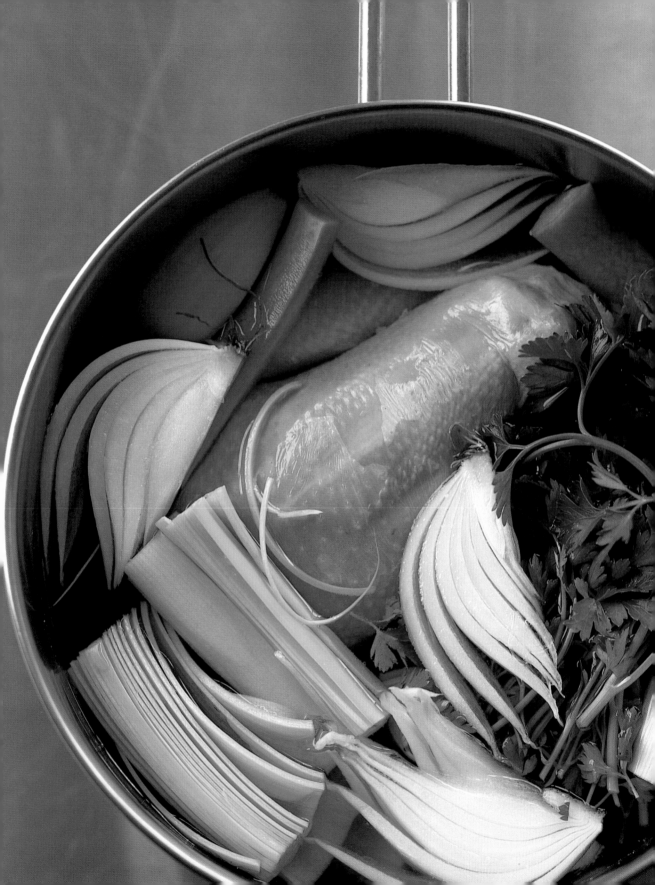

Chirpy Chicken

low carb rating:

What could be more of a pick-me-up than a mug full of this crystal-clear, energizing, healing, and immune-boosting chicken broth? In different cultures around the world, from traditional Jewish villages in frozen Siberia to the steamy humidity of the Far East, the burning heat of India or the plains of China, chicken broth functions like Jupiter: the bringer of jollity.

Serves 3
**1 leftover chicken carcass, cooked
  or uncooked**
1 leek
1 fennel bulb
**450g or 1lb organic root vegetables
  (frozen will do)**
1 large handful of mixed summer herbs

1 Trim any fat off the chicken carcass.
2 Wash and quarter the leek and fennel.
3 Wash and cut the root vegetables into large dice, if necessary.
4 Put the chicken, vegetables, and washed herbs into a large saucepan.
5 Cover with about 850ml or 30fl oz of water.
6 Simmer, covered, for forty minutes.
7 Strain off the chicken and vegetables.
8 Serve immediately.

Note This can be kept in the refrigerator for up to three days. If you do this, skim off any residue of cold fat and heat on a stove or in a microwave before serving.

vital statistics and low carb low-down

Root vegetables are an abundant source of **minerals**, **carotenoids**, and other **phytochemicals**. Although most of the **vitamin C** is lost during the prolonged cooking process, nearly all the other nutrients end up in the soup, together with the **immune-boosting** and **antiviral** components from the chicken.

Beef Tea

low carb rating:

Yes, this drink does take a long time to make, but it's well worth the effort. Not only is it a wonderfully warming and comforting beverage full of energy-boosting goodness, it's also the perfect stock for any meat stew or casserole, and served cold, it's the ideal consommé for summer. It freezes well, too, either in large containers or in ice-cube trays for times when you need small amounts of stock for cooking.

Makes 2.4 litres or 4 imperial pints
905g or 2lb stewing beef
2 carrots, washed
3 celery sticks, washed
1 large onion
3 garlic cloves
1 large rosemary stalk
4 stems of fresh sage
freshly ground black pepper

1 Remove all visible fat from the meat and cut it into cubes.
2 Put into a large saucepan, cover with water, and bring slowly to a boil.
3 Cool to allow fat to rise and skim it off.
4 Add 850ml or 30fl oz of water.
5 Chop the carrots roughly – no need to peel, top or tail if they're organic.
6 Chop the celery roughly.
7 Leave the onion and garlic whole, wash and add to the pan, along with the carrots, celery, rosemary, and sage.
8 Simmer gently for about two hours. Allow to cool before straining through muslin.
9 Reheat and season with pepper to taste.

vital statistics and low carb low-down

A mug of this tea will certainly contain more **nutrients** and **disease-fighting** natural substances than a whole meal of most hospital food. **Protein, enzymes**, and **B vitamins** from the beef are just for starters. You also get protection from the **antibacterial, antiviral,** and **antifungal** substances in onions and garlic and the **essential oils** in sage and rosemary. Light and easily digested, beef tea is one of the most **powerful** of healing drinks.

Stress Buster

low carb rating:

Taken the overnight plane? Been burning the midnight oil? Had a night on the tiles? Whatever the reason, the next day can be hell – but it needn't be. While this drink won't work miracles, it comes pretty close. The ingredients were popular with ancient Greeks and Romans, who knew that the natural oils in parsley and mint soothe the stomach and calm jangley nerves. With clear eyes, no headache, and no puffiness or gritty skin, you'll get through the day in better shape than you ever imagined possible.

Serves 2

1 medium, yellow-fleshed melon
6 mint leaves, with sprigs
6 spinach leaves, well washed
1 handful of parsley, with stems

1 Peel and deseed the melon. Wash the herbs.
2 Put all the ingredients through a juicer.
3 Mix well before serving.

vital statistics and low carb low-down
Super-rich in **potassium** and **vitamin A**. Stress Buster is a **detoxifying** juice, thanks to the parsley in its recipe. Both parsley and mint have a **healing** effect on the entire **digestive system** and are **calming** to the **central nervous system**. Melon juice also overflows with healing **betacarotenes** and is exceptionally curative and **cooling**.

Worth a Mint

low carb rating:

The sharp, almost astringent flavour of peppermint is a real eye-opener. There are, of course, many varieties of mint, probably the most popular of all culinary herbs. But peppermint has the most distinctive and unmistakable flavour. The bite of this mint tea, softened with the soothing flavour of honey, is wonderful anytime.

Serves 1

3 large sprigs of peppermint

1 tbsp runny honey

1 Wash the mint and put it into a jug or infuser.
2 Cover with 255ml or 9fl oz of boiling water.
3 Leave for ten minutes.
4 Strain into a mug or remove the central part of the infuser.
5 Add the honey and stir briskly until dissolved.

vital statistics and low carb low-down

The essential oils of **menthol** and **menthone** are found in all varieties of mint, whether it's apple mint, ginger mint, Moroccan mint or any of the dozens of their relatives. Mint is most commonly thought of as a **digestive remedy** – which indeed it is – but the **powerful** peppermint is also **protective** against infections. And it's another drink that's **very low in carbohydrates**.

Melon Days

low carb rating:

Naturopaths regard melon as a cleanser, and in Indian Ayurvedic medicine it is used as an effective diuretic. It is also cooling to the body and soothing to the digestion. The addition of watercress, broccoli, and the tart cooking apple makes this "green juice" a perfect cleanser for men, because it has a testosterone-enhancing effect. It's gently laxative, healing, a powerful immune-booster.

Serves 2
half a green melon
1 cooking apple
85g or 3oz fine broccoli florets
1 handful of watercress

1 Peel and deseed the melon.
2 Wash, core, and quarter the apple.
3 Wash the broccoli and watercress.
4 Put all the ingredients through a juicer.
5 Mix well before serving.

vital statistics and low carb low-down

Rich in **vitamins A, C, and E**. Contains **folic acid, magnesium,** and **potassium,** and has **hardly any carbs**. This juice is particularly suitable for physically **active** men who enjoy regular **sport** (of course, women can take it, too). The **mineral** content will also replace losses experienced through sweating. As a regular **cleansing** juice taken once or twice weekly, the watercress and broccoli ensure a substantial intake of **cancer-fighting nutrients**.

Skin Saver

Yes, I know. It's a pain taking the stones out of all those cherries, but it's well worth buying a cheap, easily available gadget that does the work for you, and with this recipe, you end up with the most delicious juice you've ever tasted. Do make sure you choose dessert cherries rather than the cooking variety, however, which are very sour. Buy the darkest-coloured ones you can find, as they're the richest in the highly protective natural substances.

Serves 1–2
350g or 12oz cherries
2 apples

1   Wash and stone the cherries.
2   Wash, core, and quarter the apples.
3   Put all the fruit through a juicer.
4   Stir well before serving.

vital statistics and low carb low-down
Super-rich in **vitamin C**. Rich in **carotenoids**. Contains **folic acid** and **potassium**. An added bonus of this healing juice is its huge concentration of substances called **anthocyanidins** and **proanthocyanidins** which, among other things, have powerful **protective** and **regenerative** properties directly linked to collagen that make this such **a valuable low-carb healing juice**. You won't need those injections if you consume regular amounts of Skin Saver.

Cuppa Parsley

low carb rating:

It must be an attitude unique to the British and Americans that consigns parsley to the undignified and certainly unjustified position of being little more than a decorative garnish. It's true that the European flat-leaf parsley may be slightly more chewable and palatable than the British curly variety, but both are delicious and deserve more than their usual ignominious end: the compost heap. If you're suffering the discomfort of fluid retention, this is definitely the herb for you.

Serves 1

2 heaped tsp fresh chopped parsley or 1tsp dried parsley

1 heaped tsp runny honey (preferably organic)

1. Put the parsley into an infuser or large mug.
2. Leave for ten minutes before straining.
3. Add the honey and stir vigorously.
4. Serve immediately.

vital statistics and low carb low-down

Apart from significant quantities of **vitamins A** and **C, iron, potassium,** and **calcium**, parsley has a specific medicinal property that was recognized by the ancient Greeks and Romans and used by their physicians. This herb is a **gentle** yet effective **diuretic** and a real boon to the many unfortunate women whose periods are preceded by days of painful **swollen** feet, ankles, fingers, hands, and breasts.

Sage Warmer

low carb rating:

There are endless varieties of sage, but one of my favourites is *Salvia officinalis purpurascens* – purple sage – as this has strong medicinal properties and contains significant amounts of essential oils. The most widely used culinary variety is Spanish sage, which tastes fine but contains few or no healing oils.

Serves 1
1 large sprig of sage
1/2 tsp maple syrup

1 Put the washed sage into a mug or infuser.
2 Cover with about 250ml or 9fl oz boiling water.
3 Cover and leave for ten minutes.
4 Stir in the maple syrup to serve.

vital statistics and low carb low-down

There are many natural chemicals in sage, but **thujone, cineole, borneol,** and **salviatannin** are among the most important. This is the ideal **healing** drink on a cold, raw, foggy day, as its **antiseptic** qualities protect against throat and chest infections. Gargling with sage tea is the quickest way to **relieve** the discomfort of a **sore throat**.

Seeing Red

The radish is a much overlooked and highly valuable vegetable – so valuable, in fact, that the ancient pharaohs used them (along with garlic and onions) to pay the workers who built the pyramids. A member of the cabbage family, radishes also contain cancer-fighting nutrients. The diuretic power of dandelion (or parsley) and the cleansing benefits of carrots give this healing juice a deliciously sharp and peppery flavour.

Serves 2–3

4 medium radishes

**6 carrots; peeled, topped, and tailed
    unless organic**

6 dandelion leaves

OR

a handful of parsley

1 Wash all the ingredients and put through a juicer.
2 Mix well before serving.

vital statistics and low carb low-down

Rich in **vitamin A**, **potassium**, and **sulphur**. Contains some **vitamin C** and **selenium**. Radishes **stimulate** the gall bladder to increase the release of bile and **promote** good liver function. These activities combine to make Seeing Red a real **fat-buster**, **healing**, and **cleansing** drink.

INDEX